Pocket
DUBLIN

TOP SIGHTS • LOCAL LIFE • MADE EASY

Fionn Davenport

In This Book

QuickStart Guide

Your keys to understanding the city – we help you decide what to do and how to do it

Need to Know
Tips for a smooth trip

Neighbourhoods
What's where

Explore Dublin

The best things to see and do, neighbourhood by neighbourhood

Top Sights
Make the most of your visit

Local Life
The insider's city

The Best of Dublin

The city's highlights in handy lists to help you plan

Best Walks
See the city on foot

Dublin's Best...
The best experiences

Survival Guide

Tips and tricks for a seamless, hassle-free city experience

Getting Around
Travel like a local

Essential Information
Including where to stay

Our selection of the city's best places to eat, drink and experience:

◎ Sights

✖ Eating

🍺 Drinking

★ Entertainment

🔒 Shopping

These symbols give you the vital information for each listing:

☎ Telephone Numbers
⊙ Opening Hours
P Parking
⊖ Nonsmoking
@ Internet Access
📶 Wi-Fi Access
🥗 Vegetarian Selection
👪 Family-Friendly
🐾 Pet-Friendly

🚌 Bus
⛴ Ferry
Ⓜ Metro
🚋 Tram
🚆 Train

Find each listing quickly on maps for each neighbourhood:

Bar Hemingway

16 🍺 Map p233, B2

Legend has it that Hemi self, wielding a machine ...rate this timber-pan ...ered bar during ...showpiece is a ...en by Papa ar ...town. Dress ...s.com; Hôtel Rit ... ⊙6.30pm-2a

16 🍺

6 ◎ Plac

Lonely Planet's Dublin

Lonely Planet Pocket Guides are designed to get you straight to the heart of the city.

Inside you'll find all the must-see sights, plus tips to make your visit to each one really memorable. We've split the city into easy-to-navigate neighbourhoods and provided clear maps so you'll find your way around with ease. Our expert authors have searched out the best of the city: walks, food, nightlife and shopping, to name a few. Because you want to explore, our 'Local Life' pages will take you to some of the most exciting areas to experience the real Dublin.

And of course you'll find all the practical tips you need for a smooth trip: itineraries for short visits, how to get around, and how much to tip the guy who serves you a drink at the end of a long day's exploration.

It's your guarantee of a really great experience.

Our Promise

You can trust our travel information because Lonely Planet authors visit the places we write about, each and every edition. We never accept freebies for positive coverage, so you can rely on us to tell it like it is.

The Best of Dublin 127

Dublin's Best Walks

Dublin's Best ...

Survival Guide 147

QuickStart Guide

Welcome to Dublin

Dublin is one of Europe's most enticing capitals – a drizzly dream that has captured the imaginations of virtually all who walk its mottled streets. It's a city rich in history and heritage but is equally devoted to more hedonistic endeavours: spend a couple of days or nights here and you'll soon realise that Dubliners are in deadly earnest about having fun.

Christ Church Cathedral's archway (p66)
DAVID SOANES PHOTOGRAPHY/GETTY IMAGES ©

Dublin
Top Sights

Trinity College (p24)

Ireland's most beautiful university.

National Museum of Ireland – Archaeology (p52)
Mother of all Irish museums.

Guinness Storehouse (p80)

Home of the famous beer.

© 2015 BY ENDA CAVANAGH PHOTOGRAPHY. ALL RIGHTS RESERVED

National Gallery (p54)

Art from the Middle Ages onwards.

ARTUR BOGACKI/SHUTTERSTOCK ©

Dublin Castle (p28)

Former centre of British rule.

St Patrick's Cathedral (p82)

Dublin's most important church.

ublin City Gallery – e Hugh Lane (p98)

odern art in beautiful surrounds.

Chester Beatty Library (p32)

World-class collection of books and artefacts.

hrist Church Cathedral (p66)

lying buttresses and gothic style.

Kilmainham Gaol (p84)

Former prison with a rich history.

Dublin Local Life

Local experiences and hidden gems to help you uncover the real city

Dublin is, depending on your perspective, a small city or a very large village, which makes it at once easy to navigate but difficult to understand. Spend enough time here and you'll realise exactly what we mean.

Stroll around St Stephen's Green (p34)
☑ Georgian architecture ☑ Urban greenery

ROLF G WACKENBERG/SHUTTERSTOCK ©

Temple Bar's Shopping Secrets (p68)
☑ Local markets ☑ Fashion

ander the Wilds of Phoenix Park (p94)

Green spaces ☑ Palladian architecture

Other great places to experience the city like a local:

A night out on hipster-friendly South William Street (p40)

Sunday art market at Merrion Square (p59)

Garden walks in Kilmainham (p88)

Stoneybatter style (p104)

Poolbeg Lighthouse (p116)

Brunch in Ranelagh (p124)

he Docklands' Hidden Heritage (p112)

☐ Modern architecture ☑ Beautiful bridges

Dublin
Day Planner

Day One

Start with a stroll through the grounds of **Trinity College** (p24), visiting the **Long Room** (p25) and the Book of Kells before ambling up Grafton St to **St Stephen's Green** (p38). For more beautiful books and artefacts, drop into the **Chester Beatty Library** (p32).

Pick your heavyweight institution, or visit all three: the **National Museum of Ireland – Archaeology** (p52), if only for the Ardagh Chalice and Tara Brooch; the **National Gallery** (p54), especially the Jack B Yeats room; and the **Museum of Natural History** (p57), which the kids will surely enjoy.

A night out in Temple Bar is always a bit of fun; pick a pub and let it happen.

Day Two

Begin with a little penance at Dublin's medieval cathedrals, **St Patrick's** (p82) and **Christ Church** (p6 before pursuing pleasure at the **Teeling Distillery** (p88) and then at Dublin's mc popular tourist attraction, the **Guinness Storehouse** (p80).

Go further west to Kilmainham, visiting first the fine collection at the **Irish Museum of Modern Art** (p88), and its gardens too, before going out the back entrance and stepping into **Kilmainham Gaol,** (p84) the tour of whi offers one of the most illuminating and interesting insights into Ireland's struggl for independence. If the weather is good stroll in the **War Memorial Gardens** (p8 is also recommended.

Walshe's (p107) of Stoneybatter is a superb traditional bar, full of interesting locals and hipster blow-ins looking for a 'real' Dublin experience. Alternatively, you could take in a play at e ther the **Gate** (p109) or Ireland's nationa theatre, the **Abbey** (p109). Use the Luas get you from Stoneybatter (get on at the Museum stop) and alight at Abbey St.

ort on time?

'e've arranged Dublin's must-sees into these day-by-day itineraries to make sure
u see the very best of the city in the time you have available.

ay Three

After walking the length of
O'Connell St, and pausing to
spect the bullet holes in the **General
ost Office** (p102), explore the collec-
on of the **Dublin City Gallery – Hugh
ane** (p98), including Francis Bacon's
constructed studio. The **Old Jameson
stillery** (p102), to the west in Smith-
eld, is the place to learn about (and
ste) Irish whiskey.

The collection of the **National
Museum of Ireland –
ecorative Arts & History** (p102) is
ccellent, but you'll be distracted by the
unning 18th-century barracks that is its
ome. The nearby **Arbour Hill Cemetery**
104) is where the executed leaders of
e 1916 Easter Rising are buried, while
rther west again is the broad city expanse
Phoenix Park, the largest city park in
urope.

The biggest choice of nightlife is
in the streets around **Grafton St**.
here are traditional pubs, trendy new
ars and music venues. You can drink,
lk and dance the night away, or go see
show at the **Gaiety Theatre** (p46).
hatever you choose, everything is eas-
reached in what is a pretty compact
strict.

Day Four

The award-winning **Little
Museum of Dublin** (p38) has a
wonderful collection of locally sourced
artefacts and mementos, including a
lectern used by JFK and a whole room
devoted to U2. Then, go book shopping
at the **Gutter Bookshop** (p77) in Temple
Bar or **Ulysses Rare Books** (p47), which
even has a first edition of *Ulysses*.

Saunter through the **Docklands**,
site of some of the city's brightest contemporary architecture. On a
pleasant evening, a walk to the Poolbeg
Lighthouse (p116) is well worth the effort,
if only for the splendid views of Dublin
Bay.

A visit to **O'Donoghue's** (p63) on
Merrion Row is guaranteed to be
memorable. It's a beautiful traditional bar
that is always full of revellers, and there's
a good chance there'll be a trad music
session on.

Need to Know

For more information, see Survival Guide (p147)

Currency
Euro (€)

Language
English

Visas
Not required for citizens of Australia, New Zealand, the USA or Canada, or citizens of European nations that belong to the European Economic Area (EEA).

Money
ATMs are widespread. Credit cards (with PIN) are accepted at most restaurants, hotels and shops.

Mobile Phones
All European and Australasian phones work in Dublin; some North American (non-GSM) phones don't. Check with your provider. Prepaid SIM cards cost from €10.

Time
In winter, Dublin is on GMT, also known as Universal Time Coordinated (UTC); in summer, the clock shifts to GMT plus one hour.

Tipping
Tips aren't expected in pubs unless table service is provided, then €1 for a round. Tip 10% in restaurants for decent service, up to 15% in more expensive places. Tip taxi drivers 10% or round up to the nearest euro.

① Before You Go

Your Daily Budget

Budget: Less than €150
▶ Dorm bed: €14–25
▶ Cheap meal in cafe or pub: €15–25
▶ Bus ticket: up to €2.70
▶ Some museums: free
▶ Pint: €5.50–7

Midrange: €150–€250
▶ Budget hotel double: €90–150
▶ Midrange hotel or townhouse double: €150–250
▶ Lunch or dinner in midrange restaurant: €30–40
▶ Guided tours and paid attractions: €20

Top end: More than €250
▶ Double in top-end hotel: from €250
▶ Dinner in top-end restaurant: €60–120

Websites

Dublin Tourism (www.visitdublin.com) Official website of Dublin Tourism.

Dublintown (www.dublintown.ie) Comprehensive list of events and goings on.

Lonely Planet (www.lonelyplanet.com/dublin) Destination information, hotel bookings, traveller forums and more.

Advance Planning

One month before Book accommodation, especially in summer. Book tickets for bigg live gigs.

Two weeks before Secure accommodatio in low season. Book weekend performance for main theatres, and Friday or Saturday night reservations at top-end restaurants

Three days before Book weekend tables the trendiest or most popular restaurants

2 Arriving in Dublin

...land's capital and biggest city is the most ...portant point of entry and departure for ...e country – almost all airlines fly in and ...t of Dublin Airport. The city has two ferry ...rts: the Dun Laoghaire ferry terminal and ...e Dublin Port terminal. Flights, cars and ...urs can be booked online at lonelyplanet. ...m/bookings.

At the Airport

...cated 13km north of the city centre, Dublin ...port (📞01-814 1111; www.dublinairport. ...m) has two terminals: most international ...ghts (including most US flights) use Termi-...l 2; Ryanair and select others use Terminal ...Both terminals have the usual selection of ...bs, restaurants, shops, ATMs and car-hire ...sks. Most airlines have walk-up counters ...Dublin airport; those that don't have their ...keting handled by other airlines.There is ...train service from the airport to the city ...ntre.

✈ From Dublin Airport

...estination	Best Transport
...rafton St & Around	Aircoach or taxi
...Merrion Square & ...round	Aircoach or taxi
...emple Bar	Aircoach or taxi
...ilmainham & the ...iberties	Taxi
...orth of the Liffey	Aircoach or taxi
...ocklands	Aircoach then tram or taxi

From Dublin Port

...ses from Busáras main bus terminal are ...ned to coincide with ferry arrivals and ...partures.

3 Getting Around

🚲 Bicycle

With more than 100 stations throughout the city, the rent-and-ride Dublinbikes (www. dublinbikes.ie) scheme is the ideal way to cover ground quickly.

🚌 Bus

The extensive bus system serves the whole city between 5.30am and 11.30pm but, despite bus lanes, service can be slow during busy times. You'll need exact fare or a Leap card, which is available from newsagents.

🚊 Tram

The most efficient way of getting around, but the two lines – now linked by a new line running through the city centre – are limited and serve destinations primarily south of the river and from O'Connell St east to the Docklands.

🚃 Train

The Dublin Area Rapid Transport (DART; 📞01-836 6222; www.irishrail.ie) provides quick train access to the coast as far north as Howth (about 30 minutes) and as far south as Greystones in County Wicklow.

🚗 Car & Motorcycle

Traffic in Dublin is a nightmare and parking is an expensive headache: €2.90 per hour in yellow (central) zone down to €0.60 in blue (suburban). Supervised and sheltered car parks cost around €4 per hour, with most offering a low-cost evening flat rate.

Dublin Neighbourhoods

Temple Bar (p64)
The cobbled 'cultural quarter' is popular for nights out, but the weekend markets are also a highlight.

⊙ Top Sight
Christ Church Cathedral

North of the Liffey (p96)
The city's grittier half is still full of top museums and grand Georgian architecture.

⊙ Top Sight
Dublin City Gallery – the Hugh Lane

⊙ Kilmainham Gaol

⊙ Guinness Storehouse

Christ Church Cathedral

St Patrick Cathedral

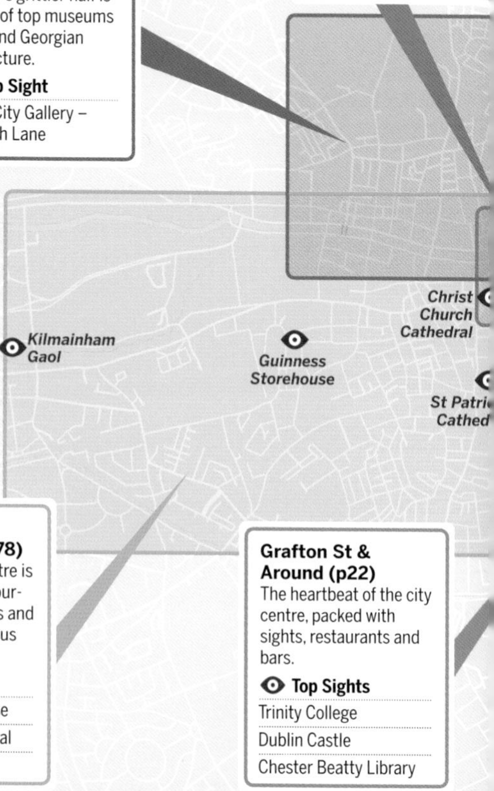

Kilmainham & the Liberties (p78)
West of the city centre is a mix of old neighbourhoods, green spaces and Ireland's most famous brewery.

⊙ Top Sights
Guinness Storehouse
St Patrick's Cathedral
Kilmainham Gaol

Grafton St & Around (p22)
The heartbeat of the city centre, packed with sights, restaurants and bars.

⊙ Top Sights
Trinity College
Dublin Castle
Chester Beatty Library

Docklands (p110)
Contemporary architecture that is the result of development since the turn of the millennium.

*Dublin City Gallery –
The Hugh Lane*

Dublin Castle

Chester Beatty Library

Trinity College

National Gallery

National Museum of Ireland – Archaeology

Merrion Square & Around (p50)
Georgian squares and public buildings, plus the country's most important museum and gallery.

⊙ Top Sights

National Museum of Ireland – Archaeology

National Gallery

The Southside (p120)
The affluent areas that border the southern bank of the Grand Canal offer tempting drinking and dining options.

Explore
Dublin

Worth a Trip

Irish Museum of Modern Art (p88)
GABRIELA INSURATELU/SHUTTERSTOCK ©

Explore

Grafton Street & Around

Pedestrianised Grafton St is the bustling heart of the city centre. You'll find the biggest range of pubs, shops and restaurants in the busy hive that surrounds it, a warren of side streets and alleys that is almost always full of people. Many of the city's most important sights and museums are here, as is Dublin's best-loved city park.

The Sights in a Day

☀️ Start with a stroll through the grounds of **Trinity College** (p24), visiting the **Old Library & Book of Kells** (p25) before ambling up Grafton St (pictured left) to **St Stephen's Green** (p38). Do a spot of retailing in **Powerscourt Townhouse Shopping Centre** (p48).

☀️ Make your way to the **Chester Beatty Library** (p32), where you can grab lunch at the excellent **Silk Road Café** (p33). After that, explore the library's beautiful books and artefacts, and then pop into the **Little Museum of Dublin** (p38).

🌙 A fine dinner at **Pichet** (p41) or the **Greenhouse** (p41), for which you'll need a reservation, and then a nightcap or more at **Kehoe's** (p42).

For a local's day strolling around St Stephen's Green, see p34.

👁️ Top Sights

Trinity College (p24)

Dublin Castle (p28)

Chester Beatty Library (p32)

🔍 Local Life

Stroll around St Stephen's Green (p34)

💛 Best of Dublin

Eating

Eatyard (p40)

Pichet (p41)

Greenhouse (p41)

Shopping

Article (p47)

Costume (p49)

Nowhere (p48)

Getting There

🚌 **Bus** All cross-city buses make their way to this part of the city.

🚋 **Tram** The Luas Green Line has its terminus at the south end of Grafton St, on the west side of St Stephen's Green.

🚶 **Walk** Grafton St is in the heart of the city and no more than 500m from all other neighbourhoods (including the western edge of the Docklands).

Top Sights
Trinity College

This calm and cordial retreat from the bustle of contemporary Dublin is Ireland's most prestigious university, a collection of elegant Georgian and Victorian buildings, cobbled squares and manicured lawns that is among the most delightful places to wander.

👁 Map p36, E1

📞 01-896 1000

www.tcd.ie

College Green

admission free

🕑 8am-10pm

🚌 all city centre

Old Library

Old Library & Book of Kells

Trinity's greatest treasures are found within the **Old Library** (www.tcd.ie; Library Sq; adult/student/family €11/9.50/22, fast-track €14/12/28; ⏰8.30am-5pm Mon-Sat, 9.30am-5pm Sun May-Sep, 9.30am-5pm Mon-Sat, noon-4.30pm Sun Oct-Apr), built by Thomas Burgh between 1712 and 1732. The star of the show is the **Book of Kells**, a breathtaking, illuminated manuscript of the four Gospels of the New Testament, created around AD 800 by monks on the Scottish island of Iona, but more stunning still is the 65m Long Room, the library's main chamber, which houses around 200,000 of the library's oldest volumes.

Other displays include a rare copy of the **Proclamation of the Irish Republic**, read out by Pádraig Pearse at the beginning of the Easter Rising in 1916, as well as the so-called **harp of Brian Ború**, which was definitely not in use when the army of this early Irish hero defeated the Danes at the Battle of Clontarf in 1014.

Front Square & Parliament Square

Through the main Regent House entrance are Front Sq and Parliament Sq, the latter dominated by the 30m-high **Campanile** (Southside), designed by Edward Lanyon and erected from 1852 to 1853 on what was believed to be the centre of the monastery that preceded the college. On your left is Richard Cassel's 18th-century **dining hall**; across from it is Sir William Chambers' **Examination Hall**, built in 1785.

Chapel

North of Parliament Sq is the 1798 **Chapel** (📞01-896 1260; ⏰8.30am-5pm, admission by special permission only), designed by William Chambers and featuring fine plasterwork by Michael Stapleton, Ionic columns and painted-glass windows. It has been

☑ Top Tips

▶ A great way to see the grounds is on a **walking tour** (Authenticity Tours; www.tcd.ie/visitors/tours; Trinity College; tours €6, incl Book of Kells €14; ⏰10.15am-3.40pm Mon-Sat, to 3.15pm Sun May-Sep, fewer midweek tours Oct & Feb-Apr; 🚌all city centre, 🚏College Green), which depart from the College Green entrance.

▶ Book a fast-track ticket online to get cheaper and speedier access to the *Book of Kells* and the Long Room.

✗ Take a Break

Take your pick from a range of sweet and savoury crêpes at **Lemon** (61 Dawson St; pancakes from €6.95; ⏰7.30am-7.30pm Mon-Wed & Fri, to 9pm Thu, 8.30am-7.30pm Sat, 9.40am-6.30pm Sun; 🚌all city centre), near the Nassau St entrance. Walk up Grafton St and head into Kehoe's (p42) for a pint.

Understand
A Catholic Ban

Trinity was exclusively Protestant until 1793, but even when the university relented and began to admit Catholics, the Catholic Church forbade it; until 1970, any Catholic who enrolled here could consider themselves excommunicated.

open to all denominations since 1972 and is only accessible by organised tour.

Fellows' Square

West of the brutalist, brilliant **Berkeley Library** (🕐closed to the public), designed by Paul Koralek in 1967, the **Arts & Social Science Building** (🕐closed to the public) is home to the **Douglas Hyde Gallery** (www. douglashydegallery.com; admission free; 🕐11am-6pm Mon-Wed & Fri, to 7pm Thu, to 4.45pm Sat; 🚇all city centre), one of the country's leading contemporary galleries. It hosts regularly rotating shows presenting the works of top-class Irish and international artists across a range of media.

Main entrance

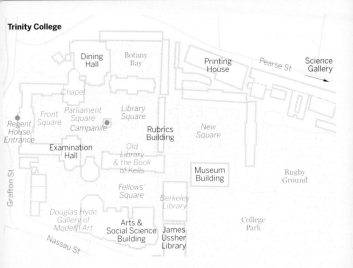

College Park

Towards the eastern end of the complex, College Park is a lovely place to lounge around on a sunny day and occasionally you'll catch a game of cricket, a bizarre sight in Ireland. Keep in mind that Lincoln Place Gate is located in the southeast corner of the grounds, providing a handy short-cut to Merrion Sq.

Science Gallery

Although it's part of the campus, you'll have to walk along Pearse St to get into Trinity's newest attraction, the **Science Gallery** (www.sciencegallery.ie; Naughton Gallery, Pearse St; admission free; ⊙exhibitions usually noon-8pm Tue-Fri, to 6pm Sat & Sun). Since opening in 2008, it has proven immensely popular with everyone for its refreshingly lively and informative exploration of the relationship between science, art and the world we live in.

Top Sights
Dublin Castle

If you're looking for a medieval castle straight out of central casting you'll be disappointed; the stronghold of British power here for 700 years is principally an 18th-century creation that is more hotchpotch palace than turreted castle.

👁 Map p36, B1

📞 01-677 7129

www.dublincastle.ie,

Dame St

guided tours adult/child €10/4, self-guided tours €7/3

🕘 9.45am-5.45pm, last admission 5.15pm

🚋 all city centre

Norman Record Tower and Chapel Royal

Guided Tours

The only way to visit the best bits of the castle is by guided tour. The 45-minute tours (departing every 20 to 30 minutes) are pretty dry, but they'll take you through the various rooms of the State Apartments including the Throne Room and St Patrick's Hall, as well the room in which the wounded James Connolly was tied to a chair while convalescing after the 1916 Easter Rising – brought back to health to be executed by firing squad. The tour also takes you below ground to the medieval undercroft.

Throne Room

Originally known as Battleaxe Hall, the Throne Room was built in 1740 as a reception room for the monarchs when they visited from London. The throne was originally presented in 1790 by William of Orange to commemorate his victory at the Battle of the Boyne and was refitted in 1821 for the visit of King George IV (the original footstool was adjusted for the visit of the diminutive Queen Victoria in 1849) and was last used by George V when he visited in 1911.

Chapel Royal

A good example of extravagant 19th-century Irish architecture, the Victorian Chapel Royal (occasionally part of the Dublin Castle tours) is decorated with more than 90 heads of various Irish personages and saints carved out of Tullamore limestone. The interior is wildly exuberant, with fan vaulting alongside quadripartite vaulting, wooden galleries, stained glass and lots of lively-looking sculpted angels.

St Patrick's Hall

The most impressive room in the whole castle is the gold-and-white-coloured St Patrick's Hall, which is used for presidential inaugurations

☑ Top Tips

▶ The only way you'll get to see the castle's most interesting bits is by guided tour.

▶ The castle is occasionally used for government functions, so parts may be closed to the public.

✗ Take a Break

Across the street from the main entrance is the Queen of Tarts (p73), a great spot for tea and cake. Leo Burdock's (p91), around the corner, is Dublin's most famous fish-and-chip shop.

and official receptions for visiting heads of state. It was built as the Lord Lieutenant's ballroom in the 1740s, although most of the decor dates from the 1790s, including the ornate ceiling triptych painted by Vincenzo Valdré (1742–1814): the three panels depict the coronation of George III, St Patrick bringing Christianity to Ireland and Henry II receiving the submission of the Irish chieftains in the 12th century.

Medieval Undercroft

The subterranean excavations of the old castle, discovered by accident in 1986, include foundations built by the Vikings (whose long-lasting mortar was made of ox blood, eggshells and horsehair), the hand-polished exterior castle walls that prevented attackers

Understand
Castle Catholics
- - - - - - - - - - - -
Until independence, Catholic Dubliners who were deemed to be too friendly with or sympathetic to the British crown were derisively termed 'Castle Catholics'.

from climbing them, the steps leading down to the moat and the trickle of the historic River Poddle, which once filled the moat on its way to join the Liffey.

Upper Yard

The Upper Yard enclosure roughly corresponds with the dimensions of the original medieval castle. On your

Dublin Castle

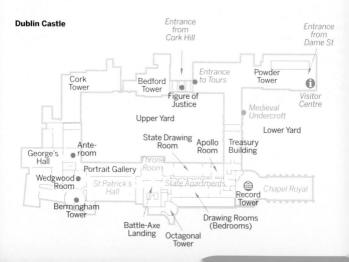

right is a Figure of Justice with her back turned to the city, reckoned by Dubliners to be an appropriate symbol for British justice. Next to it is the Bedford Tower, built in 1761 on the site of the original Norman gate. The Irish Crown Jewels were stolen from the tower in 1907 and never recovered.

The Rest of the Castle

Beside the Victorian Chapel Royal is the Norman Record Tower, the last intact medieval tower in Dublin. On your right is the Georgian Treasury Building, the oldest office block in Dublin, and behind you, yikes, is the uglier-than-sin Revenue Commissioners Building of 1960.

Top Sights
Chester Beatty Library

This world-famous library, in the grounds of Dublin Castle, houses the collection of mining engineer Sir Alfred Chester Beatty (1875–1968), bequeathed to the Irish State on his death. And we're immensely grateful for Beatty's patronage: spread over two floors, the breathtaking collection includes more than 20,000 manuscripts, rare books, miniature paintings, clay tablets, costumes and other objects of artistic, historical and aesthetic importance.

👁 Map p36, B2

📞 01-407 0750, www.cbl.ie

Dublin Castle

admission free

🕐 10am-5pm Mon-Fri, 11am-5pm Sat, 1-5pm Sun year-round, closed Mon Nov-Feb

🚌 all city centre

The Young Philatelist

Beatty's main collecting activity began in Denver between 1898 and 1905, where he amassed an impressive, prize-winning collection of stamps that chronicled the early postal history of the United States.

Art of the Book

On the 1st floor you'll find the Art of the Book, a compact but stunning collection of artworks from the Western, Islamic and East Asian worlds. Highlights include the finest collection of Chinese jade books in the world and illuminated European texts featuring exquisite calligraphy that stand up in comparison with the *Book of Kells*. Audiovisual displays explain the process of bookbinding, paper-making and printing.

Sacred Traditions

The Sacred Traditions Gallery on the 2nd floor gives a fascinating insight into the rituals and rites of passage of the major world religions – Judaism, Christianity, Islam, Buddhism and Hinduism. There are audiovisual explorations of the lives of Christ and the Buddha, as well as the Muslim pilgrimage to Mecca.

Religious Books

Its collection of Qu'rans from the 9th to the19th centuries is considered to be among the best collections of illuminated Islamic texts. You'll also find ancient Egyptian papyrus texts (including Egyptian love poems from around 1100 BC), scrolls and exquisite artwork from Burma, Indonesia and Tibet – as well as the second-oldest biblical fragment ever found (after the Dead Sea Scrolls).

☑ Top Tips

▶ There are free public tours of the museum on Wednesday at 1pm, 2pm on Saturday and Sunday at 3pm.

▶ The garden atop the building is a slice of serenity in the middle of the city.

▶ The museum hosts a series of free lunchtime talks; check the website for details.

✕ Take a Break

Lunch in the museum's **Silk Road Café** (mains €12; ⏱10am-4.45pm Mon-Fri, 11am-4.45pm Sat & Sun May-Oct, closed Mon Nov-Apr; 🚌50, 51B, 77, 78A, 123) is a gourmet treat. The excellent **Chez Max** (☎01-633 7215; www.chez-max.ie; 1 Palace St; mains €10-17; ⏱8am-midnight Mon-Fri, noon-midnight Sat & Sun; 🚌all city centre), by the main castle gate, is a fine French bistro.

Local Life
Stroll around St Stephen's Green

The most popular and best loved of the city's green spaces is St Stephen's Green, known simply as 'the green', where office workers roll up their sleeves to eat a sandwich beneath the sun at lunchtime, lovers steal a kiss on the grass and children feed clumps of bread to ever-appreciative ducks.

1 Fusilier's Arch

The main entrance to St Stephen's Green is at the top of Grafton St, via the Fusilier's Arch, modelled to look like a smaller version of the Arch of Titus in Rome. The arch commemorates the 212 soldiers of the Royal Dublin Fusiliers who were killed fighting for the British in the Boer War (1899–1902).

2 Unitarian Church

Walk down the western side of the green, past the stunning facade of the Royal College of Surgeons, the columns of which are still scarred by bullet holes from the 1916 Easter Rising. Just past it on the same side is the 1863 **Unitarian Church** (www.dublinunitarianchurch.org; 112 St Stephen's Green W; admission free; ☉worship 7am-5pm; 🚇all city centre, 🚊St Stephen's Green), a favourite with Dubliners looking to marry in accordance with a range of personal beliefs.

3 Iveagh Gardens

Cross onto Harcourt St, and walk past No 4, which was the birthplace of Sir Edward Carson, the founder of Northern Irish Unionism and the barrister who cross-examined Oscar Wilde in the libel case that preceded the infamous 1898 trial which resulted in the writer's imprisonment for homosexuality. Around the corner off Clonmel St is the little known but beautiful **Iveagh Gardens** (admission free; ☉dawn-dusk; 🚇all city centre, 🚊St Stephen's Green), designed by Ninian Niven in 1863 as the private grounds of Iveagh House.

4 Iveagh House

Walk back into St Stephen's Green and take a right along the park's southern edge, past the sculpture of James Joyce. Across the street is Iveagh House, two splendid Georgian houses that were joined by Benjamin Guinness in 1862. Number 80 (on the left) was designed by Richard Cassels in 1736. Iveagh House was gifted to the state in 1939 and is now the Department of Foreign Affairs.

5 The Three Fates

Just inside the southeastern entrance to the green is a fountain with a bronze statue in the middle, designed to represent the Three Fates. The work of artist Joseph Wackerle, it was a gift from the German people in 1956 for Ireland's role in securing foster homes for up to 500 refugee children after WWII.

6 Tonehenge

Cut through the heart of the green, visiting the 1887 bandstand (built to commemorate Queen Victoria's jubilee) and the elegant flower beds before emerging at the northeastern corner. Just by the entrance is a memorial to the victims of the Famine, but it's dwarfed by the vertical slabs that encircle the statue of Wolfe Tone – hence, the whole thing is dubbed 'Tonehenge'.

7 The Beaux Walk

Across the street, heading toward Merrion Row, is the tiny Huguenot Cemetery, established in 1693 by French Protestant refugees. All of the buildings here date from around the mid-18th century, but the ones on this corner are the most beautiful, elegant ivy-clad tributes to Georgian style. The walk back towards Grafton St used to be called the Beaux Walk, and it's still full of fancy buildings (including the Shelbourne Hotel).

For reviews see

●	Top Sights	p24
◉	Sights	p38
✕	Eating	p40
⊗	Drinking	p42
⊗	Entertainment	p44
●	Shopping	p46

Charlemont

Grand Canal

Lower Leeson St

Leeson La

E St Steph Green

S St Stephen's Green

Lower Hatch St

Earlsfort Tce

Charlemont Pl

Charlemont

Grand Pde

25 ✪

Iveagh Gardens

Upper Hatch St

Adelaide Rd

Clonmel St

Harcourt

Charlemont St

Harcourt St

Charlotte Way

Harcourt Rd

8 ✕

Charlotte St

S Richmond St

Montague St

Camden Pl

11 ✕

Camden St

Lower Camden St

Upper Camden St

Wexford St

24 ✪

23 ✕

Pleasants Pl

Grantham St

Grantham Pl

Harrington St

Lennox St

Camden Row

Pleasants St

Synge St

Lower Kevin St

New Bride St

Heytesbury St

Stamer St

Long La

McMahon St

Arnott St

Curzon St

S Circular Rd

Emor St

Victoria St

Avenue Rd

E

D

C

B

A

5

6

7

8

Sights

Green Mile
WALKING

Excellent one-hour tour of St Stephen's Green led by local historian Donal Fallon. Along the way you'll hear tales of James Joyce, the park's history and the drafting of the Irish Constitution. Book ahead as tours fill up pretty quickly. The tour also includes admission to and a guided tour of the Little Museum of Dublin (see 2 ⊚ Map p36, D4). (📞01-661 1000; www.littlemuseum.ie; Little Museum of Dublin, 15 St Stephen's Green N; adult/student €7/5; ⊙11am Sat & Sun; 🚇all city centre, 🚆St Stephen's Green)

Fab Food Trails
WALKING

Highly recommended 2½-hour tasting walks through the city centre's choicest independent producers. You'll visit up to eight bakeries, cheesemongers, markets and delis, learning about the food culture of each neighbourhood you explore. There is also a Coffee Walk (exploring the best artisanal coffee shops) and a Food & Fashion walk. Book on the website; you meet in the city centre. (www.fabfoodtrails.ie; tours €55; ⊙10am Sat)

Historical Walking Tour
WALKING

1 ⊚ Map p36, D1

Trinity College history graduates lead this 'seminar on the street' that explores the Potato Famine, Easter Rising, Civil War and Partition. Sights include Trinity, City Hall, Dublin Castle and Four Courts. In summer, themed tours on architecture, women in Irish history and the birth of the Irish state are also held. Tours depart from the College Green entrance. (📞01-878 0227; www.historicaltours.ie; Trinity College Gate; adult/student/child €12/10/free; ⊙11am & 3pm May-Sep, 11am Apr & Oct, 11am Fri-Sun Nov-Mar; 🚇all city centre)

Little Museum of Dublin
MUSEUM

2 ⊚ Map p36, D4

This award-winning museum tells the story of Dublin over the last century via memorabilia, photographs and artefacts donated by the general public. The impressive collection, spread over the rooms of a handsome Georgian house, includes a lectern used by JFK on his 1963 visit to Ireland and an original copy of the fateful letter given to the Irish envoys to the treaty negotiations of 1921, whose contradictory instructions were at the heart of the split that resulted in the Civil War. (📞01-661 1000; www.littlemuseum.ie; 15 St Stephen's Green N; adult/student €8/6; ⊙9.30am-5pm Mon-Wed & Fri, to 8pm Thu; 🚇all city centre, 🚆St Stephen's Green)

St Stephen's Green
PARK

3 ⊚ Map p36, D4

As you watch the assorted groups of friends, lovers and individuals splaying themselves across the nine elegantly landscaped hectares of Dublin's most popular green lung, St Stephen's Green, consider that those same hectares once formed a common

Domed ceiling, City Hall (p40)

for public whippings, burnings and hangings. These days, the harshest treatment you'll get is the warden chucking you off the grass for playing football or Frisbee. (⊗dawn-dusk; ⬚all city centre, ⬚St Stephen's Green)

Irish Whiskey Museum   MUSEUM

4 ⊙ Map p36, D1

If you'd like to learn more about one of Ireland's most famous tipples, spend an hour here. You'll find out why the Irish call it *uisce beatha* (water of life), how Dublin's whiskey trade collapsed and why it's on the rise again. The tour also gives you a chance to taste at least three different types of whiskey. (⌕01-525 0970; www.irishwhiskeymuseum.ie; 119

Grafton St; adult/child classic tours €17/€8.50, premium tours €20, blending experiences €28; ⊗10am-6pm; ⬚all city centre)

Bank of Ireland   NOTABLE BUILDING

5 ⊙ Map p36, D1

A sweeping Palladian pile occupying one side of College Green, this magnificent building was the Irish Parliament House until 1801 and was the first purpose-built parliament building in the world. The original building – the central colonnaded section that distinguishes the present-day structure – was designed by Sir Edward Lovett Pearce in 1729 and completed by James Gandon in 1733. (⌕01-671 1488; College Green; ⊗10am-4pm Mon-Wed & Fri, to 5pm Thu; ⬚all city centre)

Local Life

South William(sburg) St

Find an appropriate perch on South William St and watch the hipster parade go by. Good spots include the window and front bench of **Clement & Pekoe** (Map p36, C2; www.clementandpekoe.com; 50 S William St; ⏱8am-7pm Mon-Fri, 10am-6pm Sat, noon-6pm Sun; 🚌all city centre) or the outdoor seating of Grogan's Castle Lounge (p42), another favourite with the beards-and-Converse crowd. Directly opposite, the **Pygmalion** (Map p36, C2; ☎01-674 6712; www.bodytonicmusic.com; Powerscourt Townhouse Shopping Centre, 59 S William St; ⏱10am-midnight; 🚌all city centre) is also popular (especially with the younger crowd) while the more discerning hipsters can be found inside and outside Peter's Pub (p44), just to the south.

City Hall

MUSEUM

6 ◉   Map p36, B1

This beautiful Georgian structure was originally built by Thomas Cooley as the Royal Exchange between 1769 and 1779, and botched in the mid-19th century when it became the offices of the local government. Thankfully, a more recent renovation (2000) has restored it to its gleaming Georgian best. The basement has an exhibit on the city's history. (www.dublincity.ie/dublincityhall; Dame St; adult/student/child €4/2/1.50; ⏱10am-5.15pm Mon-Sat; 🚌all city centre)

Eating

Murphy's Ice Cream

ICE CREAM €

7 🍴   Map p36, C2

Get your sugar hit on with a visit to what might be the best ice-cream shop in the country. Everything is handmade with fresh ingredients from Dingle, home to the first branch of this mini-chain. Flavours rotate but the Dingle Gin ice cream is always popular and the sorbets use distilled Kerry rain. (www.murphysicecream.ie; 27 Wicklow St; scoops €2.50; ⏱noon-10pm; 🚌all city centre)

Eatyard

MARKET €

8 🍴   Map p36, C8

Spend an hour or two eating and drinking your way through a dozen or so of the city's best food vendors. There's always seasonal produce, and plenty of veggie options, as well as craft beer. The vendors rotate every few months and the market can close for a short time to accommodate this - confirm opening times online. (www.the-eatyard.com; 9-10 South Richmond St; before/after 5pm free/€2; ⏱noon-8pm Thu-Sun; 🚌14, 15, 44, 65, 140, 142 from city centre; 🚈Harcourt)

Bunsen

BURGERS €

9 🍴   Map p36, D3

Artisanal burgers that are so popular, the queues go out the door. (☎01-652 1022; www.bunsen.ie; 3 S Anne St; burgers €7-9; ⏱noon-9.30pm Mon-Wed, noon-10.30pm Thu-Sat, 1-9.30pm Sun; 🖥️all city centre, 🚇St Stephen's Green)

Pepper Pot
CAFE €

Everything is baked and made daily at the lovely cafe on the 1st-floor balcony of the Powerscourt Townhouse Shopping Centre (see 34 🔼 Map36, C2). The salads with homemade brown bread are delicious but the real treat is the soup of the day (€5.50) – the ideal liquid lunch. (www.thepepperpot.ie; mains €5-10; ⏱10am-6pm Mon-Wed & Fri, to 8pm Thu, 9am-6pm Sat, noon-6pm Sun; 🖥️all city centre)

Pichet
FRENCH €€

10 ❌ Map p36, C1

Head chef Stephen Gibson (formerly of L'Ecrivain) delivers his version of modern French cuisine to this newly refurbished dining room, whose elegance matches the fabulous food and service. Load up on an expertly made cocktail before feasting on as good a meal as you'll find at this price anywhere in the city centre. (📞01-677 1060; www.pichetrestaurant.ie; 15 Trinity St; mains €19-27; ⏱noon-3pm & 5-10pm Mon-Sat, 11am-4pm & 5-9pm Sun; 🖥️all city centre)

Hang Dai
CHINESE €€

11 ❌ Map p36, B6

You'll need a reservation to get a seat at the bar or in one of the carriage booths of this super-trendy spot, designed to look like the inside of a railway carriage. The low red lighting and soulful tunes give off the ambience of a '70s porn theatre. The food, however – contemporary versions of Chinese classics – is excellent. (📞01-545 8888; www.hangdaichinese.com; 20 Lower Camden St; mains €16-29; ⏱5pm-midnight Tue-Sat; 🖥️14, 15, 65, 83)

Pitt Bros BBQ
BARBECUE €€

12 ❌ Map p36, B2

Delicious, Southern-style barbecue – you have a choice of pulled pork, brisket, ribs, sausage or half a chicken – served amid loud music and a hipster-fuelled atmosphere that says Brooklyn, New York, rather than Birmingham, Alabama. For dessert, there's a DIY ice-cream dispenser. Locals grumble that it's a straight rip-off of Bison Bar, but the happy clientele doesn't care. (www.pittbrosbbq.com; Unit 1, Wicklow House, S Great George's St; mains €14-16; ⏱noon-midnight Mon-Fri, 12.30pm-late Sat & Sun; 🖥️all city centre)

Greenhouse
SCANDINAVIAN €€€

13 ❌ Map p36, D3

Chef Mickael Viljanen might just be the most exciting chef working in Ireland today thanks to his Scandi-influenced tasting menus, which have made this arguably Dublin's best restaurant. Wine selections are in the capable hands of Julie Dupouy, who in 2017 was voted third-best sommelier in the world, just weeks before the restaurant was awarded a Michelin star. Reservations necessary. (📞01-676 7015; www.thegreenhouserestaurant.ie; Dawson St; 2-3-course lunch menu

€29.50/38, 4-6-course dinner menu €79/95; ⊘noon-2.15pm & 6-9.30pm Tue-Sat; 🚇all city centre, 🚊St Stephen's Green)

Drinking

Kehoe's
PUB

14 🚇 Map p36, D3

This classic bar is the very exemplar of a traditional Dublin pub. The beautiful Victorian bar, wonderful snug and side room have been popular for Dubliners and visitors for generations, so much so that the publican's living quarters upstairs have since been converted into an extension – simply by taking out the furniture and adding a bar. (9 S Anne St; ⊘10.30am-11.30pm

☑ Top Tip
Music on the Streets
Grafton St is the buskers' Carnegie Hall, operating an unforgiving theory of natural selection by separating the gifted wheat from the crappy chaff.

If you insist on your own Dublin soundtrack, download these albums:

Boy (U2)

I Do Not Want What I Haven't Got (Sinéad O'Connor)

Music in Mouth (Bell X1)

Loveless (My Bloody Valentine)

Becoming a Jackal (Villagers)

Mon-Thu, to 12.30am Fri & Sat, noon-11pm Sun; 🚇all city centre)

Grogan's Castle Lounge
PUB

15 🚇 Map p36, C2

This place, known simply as Grogan's (after the original owner), is a city-centre institution. It has long been a favourite haunt of Dublin's writers and painters, as well as others from the alternative bohemian set, who enjoy a fine Guinness while they wait for that inevitable moment when they're discovered. (www.groganspub.ie; 15 S William St; ⊘10.30am-11.30pm Mon-Thu, to 12.30am Fri & Sat, 12.30-11pm Sun; 🚇all city centre)

Long Hall
PUB

16 🚇 Map p36, B2

A Victorian classic that is one of the city's most beautiful and best-loved pubs. Check out the ornate carvings in the woodwork behind the bar and the elegant chandeliers. The bartenders are experts at their craft, an increasingly rare attribute in Dublin these days. (51 S Great George's St; ⊘10.30am-11.30pm Mon-Thu, to 12.30am Fri & Sat, noon-11pm Sun; 🚇all city centre)

Chelsea Drug Store
BAR

17 🚇 Map p36, B2

It doesn't matter that its name seems plucked out of a trendy focus group and the decor carefully curated to reflect current trends (art-deco

ements, old-looking-like-new), this
s actually a beautiful bar that, at the
ime of research, was full of young
creatives ordering cocktails with
names like The Truth Behind
Augustus and Penicillin. (25 S Great
George's St; ☉4pm-midnight Mon-Fri,
noon-1.30am Sat, 4-11pm Sun; ☐all city
centre)

P.Mac's   BAR
18 🍺 Map p36, B3

This Brooklyn-style bohemian hang-
out is full of mismatched vintage
furniture, American-style pint glasses
and an alternative soundtrack veer-
ing towards the '90s. It also has
30-odd taps serving a huge variety
of craft beers. (30 Lower Stephen St;
☉noon-midnight Mon-Thu, to 1am Fri & Sat,
to 11.30pm Sun; ☐all city centre)

Mary's Bar   PUB
19 🍺 Map p36, D2

In a twist of irony, the home of the
authentic pub has seen the arrival
of a classic McPub, complete with
pseudo-old hardware shop at the front
and oak barrel tables at the back.
Utterly artificial but a popular venue;
downstairs is the even more popular
Wow Burger (www.wowburger.ie; burgers
€6-7; ☉noon-9.30pm; ☐all city centre). (8
Wicklow St; ☉11am-11.30pm Mon-Wed, to
12.30am Thu, to 1.30am Fri & Sat, noon-11pm
Sun; ☐all city centre)

Grogan's Castle Lounge

Farrier & Draper   CLUB

This relatively new venue in the
18th-century Powerscourt complex (see
34 🔴 Map36, C2) combines Prohibition-
era cool (staff in Peaky Blinders hats
and sleeve garters) and Georgian
decadence (high-vaulted ceilings, lots
of paintings on the walls). Upstairs, in
what was once Lady Powerscourt's private quarters, is a late-night bar and
club; downstairs is the beautiful Epic
Bar and, in the basement, an Italian
restaurant called La Cucina. (☎01-677
0014; www.farrieranddraper.ie; Powerscourt
Townhouse Shopping Centre, S William St;
☉noon-midnight Mon-Thu & Sun, to 2.30am
Fri & Sat; ☐all city centre)

Stag's Head

PUB

20 🍺 Map p36, C1

The Stag's Head was built in 1770, remodelled in 1895 and thankfully not changed a bit since then. It's a superb pub: so picturesque that it often appears in films and also featured in a postage-stamp series on Irish bars. A bloody great pub, no doubt. (www. louisfitzgerald.com/stagshead; 1 Dame Ct; ⏲10.30am-1am Mon-Sat, to midnight Sun; 🚆all city centre)

Peter's Pub

PUB

21 🍷 Map p36, C3

A pub for a chat and a convivial catch-up, this humble and friendly place is more like Peter's Living Room. It's one of the few remaining drinking dens in this area that hasn't changed personality in recent years, and is all the better (and more popular) for it. (☎01-679 3347; www. peterspub.ie; 1 Johnston Pl; ⏲11am-11.30pm Mon-Thu, to 12.30am Fri&Sat, 1-11pm Sun; 🚆all city centre)

George

GAY

22 🍺 Map p36, B1

The purple mother of Dublin's gay bars is a long-standing institution, having lived through the years when it was the only place in town where the gay crowd could, well, be gay. Shirley's legendary Sunday-night bingo is as popular as ever, while Wednesday's Space N Veda is a terrific night of cabaret and drag. (www.thegeorge.ie; 89 S Great George's St; weekends after 10pm €5-10, other times free; ⏲2pm-2.30am Mon-Fri, 12.30pm-2.30am Sat, 12.30pm-1.30am Sun; 🚆all city centre)

Entertainment

Devitt's

LIVE MUSIC

23 ⭐ Map p36, B6

Devitt's – aka the Cusack Stand – is one of the favourite places for the city's talented musicians to display their wares, with sessions as good as any you'll hear in the city centre. Highly recommended. (☎01-475 3414; www.devittspub.ie; 78 Lower Camden St; ⏲from 9pm Thu-Sat; 🚆14, 15, 65, 83)

Whelan's

LIVE MUSIC

24 ⭐ Map p36, B5

Perhaps the city's most beloved live-music venue is this midsize room attached to a traditional bar. This is the singer-songwriter's spiritual home: when they're done pouring out the contents of their hearts on stage, you can find them filling up in the bar along with their fans. (☎01-478 0766; www.whelanslive.com; 25 Wexford St; 🚆16, 122 from city centre)

National Concert Hall

LIVE MUSIC

25 ⭐ Map p36, D6

Ireland's premier orchestral hall hosts a variety of concerts year-round. (☎01-417 0000; www.nch.ie; Earlsfort Tce; 🚆all city centre)

Understand

The Dublin Way of Life

Dubliners are, for the most part, an informal and easygoing lot who don't stand on excessive ceremony. This doesn't mean that they don't abide by certain rules, or that there isn't a preferred way of doing things in the city.

'Slagging'

The transgressions of the unknowing are both forgiven and often enjoyed – the accidental faux pas is a great source of entertainment in a city that has made 'slagging', or teasing, a veritable art form. So, a fast, self-deprecating wit and an ability to take a joke in good spirits will win you plenty of friends. Mind you, even slagging has its hidden codes, and is only acceptable among friends: it wouldn't do at all to follow an introduction by making fun of someone's shoes!

Dublin Accents

Even in a small city like Dublin there is a lot of variation, ranging from suburban dialects that sound faintly American to working-class 'Dublinese' that is nearly incomprehensible to outsiders.

Dartspeak Aka the D4 accent (after the posh southside postal district). Borrows heavily from Home Counties British English and American English and is distinctive for its distorted vowels ('Dort' instead of 'DART') and liberal use of 'like' (pronounced 'loike') and 'right' (pronounced 'roysh').

'Inner city' accent Synonymous with working-class Dubliners. Marked by cramped vowels and words that run into each other, it is stigmatised as the uneducated accent of the city's poorer quarters, but of all the city's accents it is the closest to the earliest days of modern English and is peppered with curiously old-fashioned, high-brow words, like saying 'I was mortified' instead of 'I was embarrassed'.

Suburban accent Self-consciously clear and enunciated, this middle-class accent has its origins in the efforts of post-independence educators to foster a well-spoken accent that was deliberately 'un-British', instead filtering its clear diction and pronunciation through an Irish voice.

Gaiety Theatre

THEATRE

26 ⭐ Map p36, C3

The 'Grand Old Lady of South King St' is more than 150 years old and has for much of that time thrived on a diet of fun-for-all-the-family fare: West End hits, musicals, Christmas pantos and classic Irish plays keep the more serious-minded away, leaving more room for those simply looking to be entertained. (📞01-677 1717; www.gaietytheatre.com; S King St; ⏱7-10pm; 🚇all city centre)

Shopping

Irish Design Shop

ARTS & CRAFTS

27 🔒 Map p36, C2

Beautiful, imaginatively crafted items carefully curated by owners Clare Grennan and Laura Caffrey. If you're looking for a stylish, Irish-made memento or gift, you'll surely find it here. (📞01-679 8871; www.irishdesignshop.com; 41 Drury St; ⏱10am-6pm Mon-Wed, Fri & Sat, to 7pm Thu, 1-5pm Sun; 🚇all city centre)

Understand
Dubliners & Sport

Dubliners can tell a lot about each other based on their preferred sport and favourite teams.

Gaelic Football
Generally the preserve of the middle-class suburbs of the north side and southwest Dublin, where most of the city's clubs are located.

Football
The most popular game in Dublin has support throughout the city, primarily in working-class and middle-class neighbourhoods, where it is known as 'football'. Although the Dublin-based teams in the League of Ireland have trenchant support, your average football fan in Dublin is also a die-hard supporter of a team in the English Premier League.

Rugby
The traditional game of the city's elite – love and knowledge of rugby was a telltale indicator of privilege and elevated social status. The advent of professionalism, Ireland's repeated successes at international level and the Celtic Tiger changed all that, however, transforming rugby from an elitist pursuit to a more general expression of national pride (flavoured by the social aspirations that accompanied the disposable wealth of the Celtic Tiger years). The girls' equivalent is hockey, which is played at the most exclusive schools. But, like most sport played by girls in Dublin, it's generally out of the limelight.

Article HOMEWARES

Beautiful tableware and decorative home accessories all made by Irish designers. Ideal for unique, tasteful gifts that you won't find elsewhere. Located in the Powerscourt Townhouse Shopping Centre (see 34 🔒 Map36, C2). (📞 01-679 9268; www.articledublin.com; 1st fl, Powerscourt Townhouse Shopping Centre, S William St; ⏱10.30am-6pm Mon-Wed, Fri & Sat, to 7pm Thu, 1-5pm Sun; 🚃all city centre)

Avoca Handweavers ARTS & CRAFTS

28 🔒 Map p36, D1

Combining clothing, homewares, a basement food hall and an excellent top-floor **cafe** (mains €9-16; ⏱9.30am-5.30pm Mon-Wed & Sat, to 7pm Thu & Fri, 11am-6pm Sun), Avoca promotes a stylish but homey brand of modern Irish life – and is one of the best places to find an original present. Many of the garments are woven, knitted and naturally dyed at its Wicklow factory. There's a terrific kids' section. (📞01-677 4215; www.avoca.ie; 11-13 Suffolk St; ⏱9.30am-6pm Mon-Wed & Sat, to 7pm Thu & Fri, 11am-6pm Sun; 🚃all city centre)

Barry Doyle Design Jewellers JEWELLERY

29 🔒 Map p36, C2

Goldsmith Barry Doyle's upstairs shop is one of the best of its kind in Dublin. The handmade jewellery – using white gold, silver, and some truly gorgeous precious and semiprecious stones – is

LONELY PLANET/GETTY IMAGES ©

Sheridan's Cheesemongers (p48)

exceptional in its beauty and simplicity. Most of the pieces have Afro-Celtic influences. (📞01-671 2838; www.barrydoyledesign.com; 30 George's St Arcade; ⏱10am-6pm Mon-Wed, Fri & Sat, to 7pm Thu; 🚃all city centre)

Ulysses Rare Books BOOKS

30 🔒 Map p36, D2

Our favourite bookshop in the city stocks a rich and remarkable collection of Irish-interest books, with a particular emphasis on 20th-century literature and a large selection of first editions, including rare ones by the big guns: Joyce, Yeats, Beckett and Wilde. (📞01-671 8676; www.rarebooks.ie; 10 Duke St; ⏱9.30am-5.45pm Mon-Sat; 🚃all city centre)

Understand
Shopping for Quality

High ground rents mean that British and US chains dominate the Irish high street, especially along Grafton St and Henry St (on the other side of the Liffey just off O'Connell St). As a result, the best of the independent shops are located in the surrounding streets, where you can find high-quality, locally made goods – Irish designer clothing, handmade jewellery, unusual crafts and tasty perishables such as cheese. The best places to look:

Powerscourt Townhouse Shopping Centre Converted Georgian townhouse full of beautiful shops.

Avoca Handweavers (p47) Traditional knitwear and crafts of very high quality.

Ulysses Rare Books (p47) Literary trove of first editions.

Sheridan's Cheesemongers
FOOD

31 🔒 Map p36, D3

If heaven were a cheese shop, this would be it. Wooden shelves are laden with rounds of farmhouse cheeses, sourced from around the country by Kevin and Seamus Sheridan, who have almost single-handedly revived cheese-making in Ireland. (📞01-679 3143; www.sheridanscheesemongers.com; 11 S Anne St; ⏰10am-6pm Mon-Fri, 9.30am-6pm Sat; 🚇all city centre)

Siopaella
FASHION & ACCESSORIES

32 🔒 Map p36, C2

The popular Temple Bar shop (p77) has expanded to a new premises, which gives shoppers even bigger opportunities to nab that secondhand designer handbag at a reasonable price. (www.siopaella.com; 29 Wicklow St; ⏰10am-6pm Mon-Wed, Fri & Sat, to 7pm Thu, noon-5.30pm Sun; 🚇all city centre)

Nowhere
FASHION & ACCESSORIES

33 🔒 Map p36, B3

Men's clothing and accessories by hip designers such as CMMN_SWDN, Christopher Raeburn and A Kind of Guise. It operates an extensive online shop, too. (www.nowhere.ie; 65 Aungier St; ⏰noon-7pm Mon-Sat; 🚇all city centre)

Powerscourt Townhouse Shopping Centre
SHOPPING CENTRE

34 🔒 Map p36, C2

This absolutely gorgeous and stylish centre is in a carefully refurbished Georgian townhouse, built between 1741 and 1744. These days it's best known for its cafes and restaurants but it also does a top-end, selective

Pygmalion restaurant, Powerscourt Townhouse Shopping Centre

trade in high fashion, art, exquisite handicrafts and other chichi sundries. (📞01-679 4144; 59 S William St; 🕑10am-6pm Mon-Wed & Fri, to 8pm Thu, 9am-6pm Sat, noon-6pm Sun; 🖥all city centre)

Design Centre
CLOTHING

Mostly dedicated to Irish designer womenswear, featuring well-made classic suits, evening wear and knitwear. Irish labels include Jill De Burca, Philip Treacy, Aoife Harrison and Erickson Beamon – a favourite with Michelle Obama. Located in the Powerscourt Townhouse Shopping Centre (see **34** 🔒

Map36, C2). (📞01-679 5718; www.design centre.ie; S William St; 🕑10am-6pm Mon-Wed, Fri & Sat, to 8pm Thu; 🖥all city centre)

Costume
CLOTHING

35 🔒 Map p36, C2

Costume is considered a genuine pacesetter by Dublin's fashionistas; it has exclusive contracts with innovative designers such as Vivetta, Isabel Marant, Cedric Charlier and Zadig & Voltaire. (📞01-679 5200; www.costumedublin.ie; 10 Castle Market; 🕑10am-6pm Mon-Wed, Fri & Sat, to 7pm Thu; 🖥all city centre)

Explore

Merrion Square & Around

Georgian Dublin's apotheosis occurred in the exquisite architecture and elegant spaces of Merrion and Fitzwilliam Sqs. Here you'll find the perfect mix of imposing public buildings, museums, and private offices and residences. It is round these parts that much of moneyed Dublin works and plays, amid the neoclassical beauties erected during Dublin's 18th-century prime.

The Sights in a Day

☀️ The sizeable collection at the **National Museum of Ireland – Archaeology** (p52) is worth an entire morning, especially if you take your time with the hoard of Celtic gold and the exhibit devoted to the Stone Age 'bog bodies'. Next door is the **National Library** (p59), its beautiful main reading room open to the public.

☀️ The western side of Merrion Sq has enough cultural booty to keep you going for days. The newly restored **National Gallery** (p54) is the country's primary repository of art while, further on, the **Museum of Natural History** (p57) is a perennial favourite with anyone who loves stuffed animals and museums that have barely changed since Victorian times.

🌙 **Restaurant Patrick Guilbaud** (p60) or the **Coburg Brasserie** (p59) are the picks for those best-of-trip dinners, while a nightcap in either **Toner's** (p61) or **O'Donoghue's** (p63) makes the perfect end to the day.

👁 Top Sights

National Museum of Ireland – Archaeology (p52)

National Gallery (p54)

💜 Best of Dublin

Eating
Restaurant Patrick Guilbaud (p60)

Coburg Brasserie (p59)

L'Ecrivain (p61)

Etto (p59)

Drinking
Toner's (p61)

O'Donoghue's (p63)

House (p63)

Getting There

🚌 **Bus** Most cross-city buses will get you here (or near enough).

🚆 **Train** The most convenient DART stop is Pearse St, with the station entrance on Westland Row.

🚶 **Walk** Merrion Sq is less than 500m from St Stephen's Green (and Grafton St).

Top Sights
National Museum of Ireland – Archaeology

This is the mother of all Irish museums and the country's foremost cultural institution. One of four branches, this is the most important, home to Europe's finest selection of Bronze and Iron Age gold artefacts, the most complete collection of medieval Celtic metalwork in the world, and fascinating prehistoric and Viking relics.

👁 Map p56, A2

www.museum.ie

Kildare St

admission free

🕙 10am-5pm Tue-Sat, 2-5pm Sun

🚃 all city centre

Treasury

The Treasury is the most famous part of the collection, and its centrepieces are Ireland's best-known crafted artefacts, the **Ardagh Chalice** and the **Tara Brooch**. The 12th-century Ardagh Chalice is made of gold, silver, bronze, brass, copper and lead; it measures 17.8cm high and 24.2cm in diameter and, put simply, is the finest example of Celtic art ever found. The equally renowned Tara Brooch was crafted around AD 700, primarily in white bronze, but with traces of gold, silver, glass, copper, enamel and wire beading, and was used as a clasp for a cloak.

Ór-Ireland's Gold

Elsewhere in the Treasury is the Ór-Ireland's Gold exhibition, featuring stunning jewellery and decorative objects created by Celtic artisans in the Bronze and Iron Ages. Among them are the **Broighter Hoard**, which includes a 1st-century-BC large gold collar, unsurpassed anywhere in Europe, and an extraordinarily delicate gold boat. There's also the wonderful **Loughnasade bronze war trumpet**, which also dates from the 1st century BC. It is 1.86m long and made of sheets of bronze, riveted together, with an intricately designed disc at the mouth.

Kingship & Sacrifice

The collection of Iron Age 'bog bodies' – four figures in varying states of preservation dug out of the midland bogs – is a museum showstopper. The accompanying detail that will make you pause: scholars now believe that all of these bodies were victims of the most horrendous ritualistic torture and sacrifice – the cost of being notable figures in the Celtic world.

☑ Top Tips

▶ If you don't mind groups, the themed guided tours will help you wade through the myriad of exhibits.

▶ If you want to avoid crowds, the best time to visit is weekday afternoons, when school groups have gone, and never during Irish school holidays.

✕ Take a Break

Head to the museum's excellent **Brambles** (mains around €7; ◷10am-4pm Mon, 10am-5pm Tue-Sat, noon-5pm Sun; 🖵all city centre) cafe for good salads, sandwiches and hot dishes. Go around the corner to the **Shelbourne** (☎01-676 6471; www.theshelbourne. ie; 27 St Stephen's Green N; r from €385; 🅿@🛜; 🖵all city centre, 🖵St Stephen's Green) for afternoon tea or a drink in the Horse-shoe Bar.

Top Sights
National Gallery

A stunning Caravaggio and a room full of Ireland's pre-eminent artist, Jack B Yeats, are just a couple of highlights from this fine collection.

Its original assortment of 125 paintings has grown, mainly through bequests, to more than 13,000 artworks, including oils, watercolours, sketches, prints and sculptures.

⊙ Map p56, B2

www.nationalgallery.ie

West Merrion Sq

admission free

⊙ 9.15am-5.30pm Mon-Wed, Fri & Sat, to 8.30pm Thu, 11am-5.30pm Sun

🚌 4, 7, 8, 46A from city centre

The Taking of Christ

The absolute star exhibit from a pupil of the European schools is Caravaggio's sublime *The Taking of Christ,* in which the troubled Italian genius attempts to light the scene figuratively and metaphorically (the artist himself is portrayed holding the lantern on the far right). Fra Angelico, Titian and Tintoretto are all in this neighbourhood.

The Yeats Room

More than 30 paintings by Jack B Yeats, a uniquely Irish impressionist and arguably the country's greatest artist. Some of his finest moments are *The Liffey Swim, Men of Destiny* and *Above the Fair.*

The Vaughan Collection

One of the most popular exhibitions occurs only in January, when the gallery hosts its annual display of the Vaughan Collection, featuring watercolours by Joseph Turner. The 35 works in the collection are best viewed at this time due to the particular quality of the winter light.

Other Paintings

Facing Caravaggio, way down the opposite end of the gallery, is *A Genovese Boy Standing on a Terrace* by Van Dyck. Old Dutch and Flemish masters line up in between, but all defer to Vermeer's *A Lady Writing a Letter,* which is lucky to be here at all, having been stolen by Dublin gangster Martin Cahill in 1992, as featured in the film *The General.*

☑ **Top Tips**

▶ The best time to visit the gallery is Thursday evening, when it's open late and there's fewer visitors.

▶ There are family workshops for kids to try their hand at art throughout the year, usually on Saturdays; check the gallery website for details.

✕ **Take a Break**

Marcel's (p60) on Merrion Row is great for a classy lunch. Drop into Doheny & Nesbitt's (p63) for a post-gallery pint and a chat.

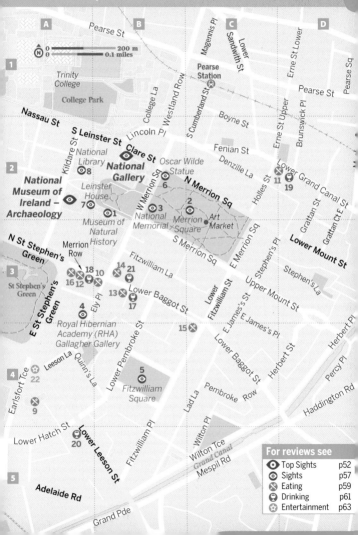

N
0 — 200 m
0 — 0.1 miles

Trinity
College

College Park

Pearse St

Magennis Pl

Lower
Sandwith St

Pearse
Station

Pearse St

Erne St Lower

Pearse St

Nassau St

S Leinster St

Kildare St

College La

Westland Row

Lincoln Pl

Clare St

S Cumberland St

Boyne St

Erne St Upper

Brunswick Pl

National
Library
⊙ 8

National
Gallery

Oscar Wilde
Statue
⊙ 6

Fenian St

Denzille La

Holles St

N Merrion Sq

Lower Grand Canal St
♙ 11   ♙ 19

National
Museum of
Ireland –
Archaeology ⊙

Leinster
House

⊙ 7   ⊙ 1

Museum of
Natural
History

W Merrion Sq

⊙ 3

National
Memorial

N Merrion Sq

⊙ 2

Merrion
Square

● Art
Market

E Merrion Sq

Grattan St

Grattan Ct

Lower Mount St

N St Stephen's
Green

Merrion
Row

S Merrion Sq

St Stephen's
Green

E St Stephen's
Green

✕ 16   ⊙ 18   ⊙ 10
✕ 12

Fitzwilliam La

✕ 14   ⊙ 21

Fitzwilliam St

Stephen's Pl

Upper Mount St

Stephen's La

⊙ 4

Ely Pl

⊙ 13   ⊙ Lower Baggot St
        ♙ 17

Lower
Fitzwilliam St

E James's St

E James's Pl

Royal Hibernian
Academy (RHA)
Gallagher Gallery

Leeson La

Quinn's La

Lower Pembroke St

Pembroke St

✕ 15

Lower Baggot St

Herbert St

Herbert Pl

Percy Pl

Earlsfort Tce

★ 22

✕ 9

⊙ 5

Fitzwilliam
Square

Lad La

Pembroke Row

Haddington Rd

Lower Hatch St

♙ 20

Lower Leeson St

Fitzwilliam Pl

Wilton Pl

Wilton Tce

Grand Canal

Mespil Rd

Adelaide Rd

Grand Pde

For reviews see	
⊙ Top Sights	p52
⊙ Sights	p57
✕ Eating	p59
♙ Drinking	p61
★ Entertainment	p63

Oscar Wilde statue by Danny Osborne (p58)

Sights

Museum of Natural History
MUSEUM

1 ⊙ Map p56, B2

Dusty, weird and utterly compelling, this window into Victorian times has barely changed since Scottish explorer Dr David Livingstone opened it in 1857 – before disappearing into the African jungle for a meeting with Henry Stanley. It is a fine example of Victorian charm and scientific wonderment, and its enormous collection is a testament to the skill of taxidermy. (National Museum of Ireland – Natural History; www.museum.ie; Upper Merrion St; admission free; ☉10am-5pm Tue-Sat, 2-5pm Sun; 🚌7, 44 from city centre)

Merrion Square
PARK

2 ⊙ Map p56, C2

Merrion Sq is the most prestigious and, arguably, the most elegant of Dublin's Georgian squares. Its well-kept lawns and tended flower beds are flanked on three sides by gorgeous Georgian houses with colourful doors, peacock fanlights, ornate door knockers and, occasionally, foot-scrapers, used to remove mud from shoes. Over the last two centuries they've been used by some notable residents. (☉dawn-dusk; 🚌all city centre)

Top Tip

Art in January

The Vaughan Collection of watercolours by JMW Turner at the National Gallery (p54) is only displayed during the month of January, when the light is just right to appreciate the delicacy and beauty of these masterpieces.

National Memorial   MEMORIAL

3 ◉ Map p56, B2

The National Memorial is a pyramid-shaped stone-and-glass sculpture designed by Brian King (1942–2017) and unveiled by the then-president Mary McAleese in 2008. Inside are four bronze figures, representing the various branches of the Defense Forces, keeping watch over an eternal flame lit to commemorate those who died serving Ireland. (Merrion Sq W; ⏲24hr; 🚍all city centre)

Royal Hibernian Academy (RHA) Gallagher Gallery   GALLERY

4 ◉ Map p56, A3

This large, well-lit gallery at the end of a serene Georgian street has a grand name to fit its exalted reputation as one of the most prestigious exhibition spaces for modern and contemporary art in Ireland. Its exhibitions are usually of a very high quality, and well worth a visit. (📞01-661 2558; www.rhagallery.ie; 15 Ely Pl; admission free; ⏲11am-5pm Mon, Tue & Thu-Sat, to 8pm Wed, noon-5pm Sun; 🚍10, 11, 13B, 51X from city centre)

Fitzwilliam Square   PARK

5 ◉ Map p56, B4

The smallest of Dublin's great Georgian squares was completed in 1825. William Dargan (1799–1867), the railway pioneer and founder of the National Gallery, lived at No 2, and the artist Jack B Yeats (1871–1957) lived at No 18. In 2017 it began hosting a summer market of more than a dozen vendors. (⏲closed to public; 🚍10, 11, 13B, 46A from city centre)

Oscar Wilde Statue   STATUE

6 ◉ Map p56, B2

Just inside the northwestern corner of Merrion Sq is a flamboyant statue of Oscar Wilde, who grew up across the street at No 1 (now used exclusively by the American University Dublin); Wilde wears his customary smoking jacket and reclines on a rock. Atop one of the plinths, daubed with witty one-liners and Wildean throwaways, is a small green statue of Oscar's pregnant mother. (Merrion Sq; ⏲dawn-dusk; 🚍7, 8 & 46A from city centre)

Leinster House   NOTABLE BUILDING

7 ◉ Map p56, A2

All the big decisions are made at the Oireachtas (parliament). This Palladian mansion was built as a city residence for James Fitzgerald, the Duke of Leinster and Earl of Kildare, by Richard

Cassels between 1745 and 1748. Prearranged free **guided tours** (🕙10.30am, 11.30am, 2.30pm & 3.30pm Mon-Fri) are available when parliament is in session (but not sitting); entry tickets to the observation galleries are available. (Oireachtas Éireann; 🖉01-618 3271; www.oireachtas.ie; Kildare St; 🕙observation galleries 2.30-8.30pm Tue, 10.30am-8.30pm Wed, 10.30am-5.30pm Thu Nov-May; 🚇all city centre)

National Library   HISTORIC BUILDING

8 ◉ Map p56, A2

Suitably sedate and elegant, the National Library was built from 1884 to 1890 by Sir Thomas Newenham Deane, to a similar design as the National Museum of Ireland – Archaeology. Its extensive collection has many valuable early manuscripts, first editions and maps. Parts of the library are open to the public, including the domed reading room where Stephen Dedalus expounded his views on Shakespeare in James Joyce's *Ulysses*. There's a **Genealogy Advisory Service** (🖉01-603 0256; 🕙9.30am-5pm Mon-Wed, to 4.45pm Thu & Fr) on the 2nd floor. (www.nli.ie; Kildare St; admission free; 🕙9.30am-7.45pm Mon-Wed, to 4.45pm Thu & Fri, 9.30am-12.45pm Sat; 🚇all city centre)

Eating

Coburg Brasserie   FRENCH €€

9 ✖ Map p56, A4

The French-inspired, seafood-leaning cuisine at this revamped hotel brasserie puts the emphasis on shellfish: the all-day menu offers oysters, mussels and a range of 'casual' lobster dishes, from lobster rolls to lobster cocktail. The bouillabaisse is chock-full of sea flavours, and you can also get a shrimp burger and a fine plate of Connemara whiskey-cured organic salmon. Top-notch. (🖉01-602 8900; www.thecoburgdublin.com; Conrad International, Earlsfort Tce; mains €11-18; 🚇all city centre)

Etto   ITALIAN €€

10 ✖ Map p56, B3

Award-winning restaurant and wine bar that does contemporary versions of classic Italian cuisine. All the ingredients are fresh, the presentation is exquisite and the service is just right. Portions are small, but the food is so rich you won't leave hungry. The only downside is the relatively quick turnover; lingering over the excellent wine would be nice. Book ahead.

◯ Local Life
Sunday Painters

On Sunday, the wrought-iron fences of Merrion Sq convert to gallery walls for the traditional open-air **art market** (Map p56, B2; www.merrionart.com; Merrion Sq; 🕙10am-dusk Sun; 🚇all city centre). At any given time you'll find the work of 150 artists, mostly Sunday-painter types with a penchant for landscapes and still lifes, some of whom are very talented indeed.

☑ Top Tip

Budget Michelin

L'Ecrivain's lunch special is a three-course tasting menu for €45; Restaurant Patrick Guilbaud has a two-/three course lunch for €50/60. Book ahead for both.

(☎01-678 8872; www.etto.ie; 18 Merrion Row; mains €18-23; ⊙noon-10pm Mon-Fri, 12.30-10pm Sat; ☐all city centre)

House
MEDITERRANEAN €€

This gorgeous bar (see **20** ☐ Map p56, A5) does a limited selection of main courses, but the real treats are the tapas-style sharing plates, including wild mushroom risotto and pulled pork, grilled halloumi and salt and pepper calamari. (www.housedublin.ie; 27 Lower Leeson St; tapas €9-11, mains €14-26; ⊙8am-midnight Mon-Wed, 8am-3am Thu & Fri, 4pm-3am Sat; ☐11, 46, 118, 145)

Musashi Hogan Place
JAPANESE €€

11 ☒ Map p56, D2

The third branch of the expanding Musashi empire, serving the same excellent and authentic sushi, sashimi and maki as the original **restaurant** (☎01-532 8057; www.musashidublin.com; 15 Capel St; mains €13-19; ⊙noon-10pm; ☐all city centre, ☐Jervis) on the north side of the Liffey. (☎01-441 0106; www. musashidublin.com; 48 Hogan Pl; sushi €3-4, maki rolls €7-8, mains €14-16; ⊙noon-10pm Sun-Thu, to 11pm Fri & Sat; ☐4, 7 from city centre)

Marcel's
FRENCH €€

12 ☒ Map p56, A3

An elegant brasserie with Hermès orange-coloured chairs, blue-and-white Churchill china and superb, French-inspired cuisine – just the way they'd eat it in New York. It's owned by the same crowd as the **Green Hen** (☎01-670 7238; www.thegreenhen.ie; 33 Exchequer St; mains €20-30; ⊙noon-11pm; ☐all city centre), and the similarities are obvious and complementary. To one side is a bar – done in traditional Irish style. Bookings recommended. (☎01-660 2367; www.marcels.ie; 13 Merrion Row; mains €20-32, 3-course menu €50; ⊙noon-3pm & 5-10pm Sun-Thu, noon-11pm Fri-Sat; ☐all city centre)

Xico
MEXICAN €€

13 ☒ Map p56, B3

It's quite the scene at this under-ground Mexican restaurant, where the music is loud and the food – tacos, tostadas and main courses such as tuna ceviche and a fine chilli bowl – is washed down with margaritas. Yes, it's a restaurant, but you'd better be in the mood for a fiesta. (www.xico.ie; 143 Lower Baggot St; mains €10-18; ⊙5pm-midnight Mon-Sat; ☐all city centre)

Restaurant Patrick Guilbaud
FRENCH €€€

14 ☒ Map p56, B3

Ireland's only Michelin two-star is understandably considered the best in the country by its devotees, who proclaim Guillaume Lebrun's French haute cuisine the most exalted expression of the culinary arts. If you like formal dining, this is as good as it gets: the lunch menu is an absolute steal, at least in this stratosphere. Innovative and beautifully presented. (☑01-676 4192; www.restaurantpatrickguil baud.ie; 21 Upper Merrion St; 2-/3-course set lunch €50/60, dinner menus €90-185; ⊕12.30-2.30pm & 7.30-10.30pm Tue-Sat; ☑7, 46 from city centre)

L'Ecrivain
FRENCH €€€

15 🍴 Map p56, C4

Head chef Derry Clarke is considered a gourmet god for the exquisite simplicity of his creations, which put the emphasis on flavour and the best local ingredients – all given the French once over and turned into something that approaches divine dining. The Michelin people like it too and awarded it one of their stars. (☑01-661 1919; www.lecrivain.com; 109a Lower Baggot St; 3-course lunch menus €45, 8-course tasting menus €90, mains €45; ⊕12.30-2pm Wed-Fri, 6.30-10pm Mon-Sat; ☑38, 39 from city centre)

Bang Café
MODERN EUROPEAN €€€

16 🍴 Map p56, A3

Fashionistas and foodies have long been aficionados of this stylish spot, which turns out top-notch contemporary Irish fare, including Slaney lamb rump and free-range Challans duck. The two-course pre-theatre menu (€26) is a good deal and is available all night Sunday to Wednesday

Trad music session, O'Donoghue's (p63)

(until 6.30pm Thursday to Saturday). (☑01-400 4229; www.bangrestaurant.com; 11 Merrion Row; mains €24-33; ⊕5.30-10pm Mon-Thu, to 11pm Fri & Sat, to 9.30pm Sun; ☑all city centre)

Drinking

Toner's
PUB

17 🍺 Map p56, B3

Toner's, with its stone floors and antique snugs, has changed little over the years and is the closest thing you'll get to a country pub in the heart of the city. Next door, Toner's Yard is a comfortable outside space. The shelves and drawers are reminders that it once doubled as a grocery

Understand

Traditional & Folk Music

Irish music – commonly referred to as 'traditional' or simply 'trad' – has retained a vibrancy not found in other traditional European forms. This is probably because, although Irish music has retained many of its traditional aspects, it has itself influenced many forms of music, most notably US country and western – a fusion of Mississippi Delta blues and Irish traditional tunes that, combined with other influences like gospel, is at the root of rock and roll. Another reason for its current success is the willingness of its exponents to update the way it's played – in ensembles rather than the customary *céilidh*.

The pub session is still the best way to hear the music at its rich, lively best – and thanks largely to the tourist demand, there are some terrific sessions in pubs throughout the city. Thankfully, though, the best musicians have also gone into the recording studio. If you want to hear musical skill that will both tear out your heart and restore your faith in humanity, go no further than the fiddle-playing of Tommy Peoples on *The Quiet Glen* (1998), the beauty of Paddy Keenan's uillean pipes on his self-titled 1975 album, or the stunning guitar playing of Andy Irvine on albums such as *Compendium: The Best of Patrick Street* (2000).

The most famous traditional band is The Chieftains, who spend most of their time these days playing in the US. More folksy than traditional were The Dubliners, founded in O'Donoghue's on Merrion Row the same year as The Chieftains. Most of the original members, including the utterly brilliant Luke Kelly and fellow frontman Ronnie Drew, have died, but the group still plays the odd nostalgia gig.

Another band whose career has been stitched into the fabric of Dublin life is The Fureys, comprising four brothers from the travelling community along with guitarist Davey Arthur. And if it's rousing renditions of Irish rebel songs you're after, you can't go past The Wolfe Tones. Ireland is packed with traditional talent and we strongly recommend that you spend some time in a specialised shop such as Claddagh Records, which has branches on Cecilia St in Temple Bar and Westmoreland St.

Since the 1970s various bands have tried to blend traditional with more progressive genres, with mixed success. The first band to pull it off was Moving Hearts, led by Christy Moore, who went on to become an important folk musician in his own right.

shop. (☎01-676 3090; www.tonerspub.ie; 139 Lower Baggot St; ⊙10.30am-11.30pm Mon-Thu, to 12.30am Fri & Sat, 11.30am-11pm Sun; ☒7, 46 from city centre)

O'Donoghue's PUB

18 ☻ Map p56, A3

The pub where traditional music stalwarts The Dubliners made their name in the 1960s still hosts live music nightly, but the crowds would gather anyway – for the excellent pints and superb ambience, in the old bar or the covered coach yard next to it. (www.odonoghues.ie; 15 Merrion Row; ⊙10.30am-11.30pm Mon-Thu, to 12.30am Fri & Sat, noon-11pm Sun; ☒all city centre)

Square Ball BAR

19 ☻ Map p56, D2

This bar is many things to many people: craft beer and cocktail bar in front, sports lounge and barbecue pit in the back and an awesome vintage arcade upstairs. There are also plenty of board games, so bring your competitive spirit. (☎01-662 4473; www.the-square-ball.com; 45 Hogan Pl; ⊙4-11.30pm Mon, noon-11.30pm Tue-Thu, noon-12.30am Fri & Sat, noon-11pm Sun; ☒4, 7 from city centre)

House BAR

20 ☻ Map p56, A5

Spread across two Georgian townhouses, this could be Dublin's most beautiful modern bar, with gorgeous wood-floored rooms, comfortable couches and even log fires in winter to amp up the cosiness. In the middle there's a lovely glassed-in outdoor space that on a nice day bathes the rest of the bar with beautiful natural light. There's also an excellent menu. (☎01-905 9090; www.housedublin.ie; 27 Lower Leeson St; ⊙8am-midnight Mon-Wed, 8am-3am Thu & Fri, 4pm-3am Sat; ☒11, 46, 118, 145)

Doheny & Nesbitt's PUB

21 ☻ Map p56, B3

A standout, even in a city of wonderful pubs, Nesbitt's is equipped with antique snugs and is a favourite place for the high-powered gossip of politicians and journalists; Leinster House is only a short stroll away. (☎01-676 2945; www.dohenyandnesbitts.ie; 5 Lower Baggot St; ⊙10am-11.30pm Mon-Thu, 10am-2am Fri & Sat, noon-11pm Sun; ☒all city centre)

Entertainment

Sugar Club LIVE MUSIC

22 ✿ Map p56, A4

There's live jazz, cabaret and soul music on weekends in this comfortable theatre-style venue on the corner of St Stephen's Green. (☎01-678 7188; www.thesugarclub.com; 8 Lower Leeson St; €7-20; ⊙7pm-late; ☒7, 46 from city centre)

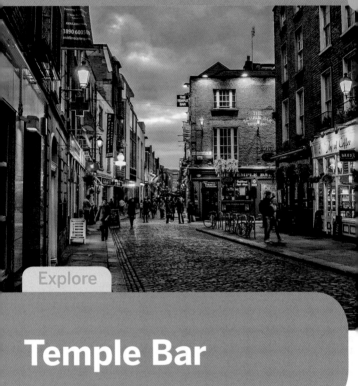

Explore

Temple Bar

Dublin's best-known district is the cobbled playpen of Temple Bar, where mayhem and merriment is standard fare, especially on summer weekends when the pubs are full and the party spills out onto the streets. During daylight hours there are shops and galleries to discover, which at least lend some truth to the area's much-mocked title of 'cultural quarter'.

The Sights in a Day

☀ During the day, Temple Bar is a browser's experience. There's always something happening on either **Meeting House Square** or **Temple Bar Square**, whether it's a street performer or – at weekends – a **food market** (p69) and a **book fair** (p69). Be sure to grab the ubiquitous snap of the **Ha'Penny Bridge** (p73).

☀ After lunch – **Banyi Japanese Dining** (p74) is the best Japanese restaurant in town – you should check out the latest exhibition at the **Gallery of Photography** (p72) and explore the **National Photographic Archive** (p72) just across the square. Check out **Gutter Bookshop** (p77) – locally owned and one of the friendliest bookshops in town.

☾ Dublin's one-time party zone still likes to have a good time, and is definitely at its most animated in the evenings, when you have the choice of a traditional music session at the **Auld Dubliner** (p75) or a rock gig at the **Workman's Club** (p76), some decent clubbing at **Mother** (p76) – Saturdays only – or an old-fashioned cocktail at the **Liquor Rooms** (p74).

For a local's day shopping in Temple Bar, see p68.

Top Sight

◉ Christ Church Cathedral (p66)

Local Life

Temple Bar's Shopping Secrets (p68)

Best of Dublin

Drinking & Nightlife
Vintage Cocktail Club (p75)

Temple Bar (p75)

Liquor Rooms (p74)

Shopping
Temple Bar Food Market (p69)

Gutter Bookshop (p77)

Claddagh Records (p77)

Siopaella Design Exchange (p69)

Lucy's Lounge (p77)

Getting There

🚌 **Bus** As Temple Bar is right in the heart of the city, all cross-city buses will deposit you by the cobbled, largely pedestrianised streets, making access – and escape – that bit easier.

🚶 **Walk** Temple Bar is easily accessible on foot from Grafton St to the southeast, Kilmainham to the west and the north side of the river to the north.

Top Sights
Christ Church Cathedral

Its hilltop location and eye-catching flying buttresses make this the most photogenic of Dublin's three cathedrals as well as one of the capital's most recognisable symbols.

◉ Map p70, A4

www.christchurchcathedral.ie

Christ Church Pl; adult/
student/child €6.50/4/2.50,
with Dublinia €14.50/12/7.50

◷ 9am-5pm Mon-Sat, 12.30-
2.30pm Sun year-round,
longer hours Mar-Oct

🚌 50, 50A, 56A from Aston
Quay, 54, 54A from Burgh Quay

Guided Tour

Guided tours (adult/family €4/12; ⏱12.10pm, 2pm & 4pm Mon-Fri, 2pm, 3pm & 4pm Sat) include the belfry, but you'll need to be on the specialist belfry tour (11.30am and 1.15pm Saturday, 1.15pm Sunday) to hear the campanologist explain the art of bell-ringing and have a go yourself.

Strongbow Monument

The armoured figure on the tomb is unlikely to be of Strongbow (it's more probably the Earl of Drogheda), but his internal organs may have been buried here. A popular legend relates an especially visceral version of the daddy-didn't-love-me tale: the half-figure beside the tomb is supposed to be Strongbow's son, who was cut in two by his loving father when his bravery in battle was suspect – an act that surely would have saved the kid a fortune in therapist's bills.

Tomb of the Earl of Kildare

The south transept contains the super baroque tomb of the 19th Earl of Kildare, who died in 1734. His grandson, Lord Edward Fitzgerald, was a member of the United Irishmen and died in the abortive 1798 Rising.

The Crypt

Curiosities in the crypt include a glass display case housing a mummified cat in the act of chasing a mummified rat (aka Tom and Jerry), frozen midpursuit inside an organ pipe in the 1860s.

☑ **Top Tips**

▶ The combination ticket that includes Dublinia is good value if you're visiting with kids.

▶ The cathedral has a weekly schedule of sung masses, which can be very beautiful; check the website for details.

✖ **Take a Break**

The Queen of Tarts (p73), with two locations around the corner from each other, does lovely cakes and coffee. Take your pick from Temple Bar's collection of pubs, but the Temple Bar (p75) is a classic.

Local Life
Temple Bar's Shopping Secrets

Temple Bar is Dublin's main tourist hot spot, so it's often hard to find the more authentic experiences among its sea of plastic paddy tourism. But the cobbled streets do have plenty to offer in terms of retail, including lots of locally made, locally sourced items you can wear or eat.

1 Crown Alley

Just behind the Central Bank, Crown Alley stretches northward to Temple Bar Sq. Take a look at the huge art nouveau–style mural on the gable wall of Bloom's Hotel, featuring Leopold Bloom and Buck Mulligan from Joyce's *Ulysses*. On your left towards the bottom of the street is the Bad Ass Cafe, which employed the young Sinéad O'Connor as a waiter.

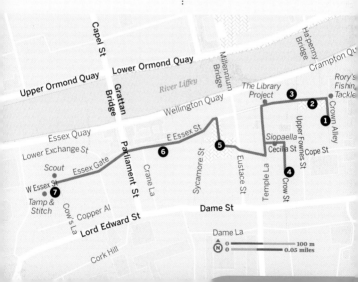

❷ Temple Bar Square

On weekends the square hosts a **book fair** (Map p70, D2; ⊙11am-6pm Sat & Sun; 🖳all city centre), and there's usually musical accompaniment which gives a terrific atmosphere as people sit at the outdoor cafes and let the show unfold.

❸ Temple Bar

The street, rather than the neighbourhood, runs east–west along the square's northern edge. Buy fishing tackle in **Rory's Fishing Tackle** (www.rorys.ie; 17a Temple Bar; ⊙9.30am-6pm Mon-Sat, noon-5pm Sun; 🖳all city centre), peruse contemporary art in the **Temple Bar Gallery & Studios** (🗐01-671 0073; www.templebargallery.com; 5 Temple Bar; admission free; ⊙11am-6pm Tue-Sat; 🖳all city centre) and check out photography from all over the world at the **Library Project** (http://tlp.photoireland.org; 4 Temple Bar; ⊙11am-6pm Mon-Fri, noon-6pm Sat & Sun; 🖳all city centre).

❹ Crow Street

This is one of Temple Bar's genuinely alternative streets. On one side is **All City Records** (4 Crow St; ⊙11am-7pm Mon-Wed, Fri & Sat, to 8pm Thu, noon-6pm Sun; 🖳all city centre), one of the best in town for dance music. On the northwestern corner is part of the growing **Siopaella** (Map p70, D2; www.siopaella.com; 25 Temple Lane S; ⊙noon-6pm Mon-Wed, Fri & Sat, to 7pm Thu; 🖳all city centre) empire.

❺ Meeting House Square

From Cecilia St, head west, through Curved St and down into Meeting House Sq, which on Saturdays is home to the **Temple Bar Food Market** (Map p70, C2; www.facebook.com/TempleBarFood-Market; ⊙10am-5pm Sat; 🖳all city centre), the best gourmet market in Dublin. You can buy everything from sushi to salsa, and all the vendors proudly display their organic, local credentials. On Sundays in summer, the square gives over to regular free concerts.

❻ Essex Street East

Walk west along Essex St, past **Connolly Books** (🗐01-670 8707; www.communistpartyofireland.ie/cbooks; 43 Essex St E; ⊙9.30am-6pm Mon-Sat; 🖳all city centre), a bookshop with a leftist lean just below the **New Theatre** (🗐01-670 3361; www.thenewtheatre.com; 43 Essex St E; adult/concession €16/12.50; ⊙shows 7.30pm Mon-Fri, 2.30pm & 7.30pm Sat; 🖳all city centre), which does all kinds of experimental theatre. Across the street is the Clarence Hotel, owned by U2, although it's been some years since any of the lads have been seen there.

❼ Old City

Cross Parliament St and you're now in Old City, named because the western end of Temple Bar is roughly where Viking Dublin was. Ironically, the area's newest, hippest boutiques are all here, including **Scout** (www.scoutdublin.com; 5 Smock Alley Ct, Essex St W; ⊙10.30am-6pm Mon-Wed, Fri & Sat, to 7pm Thu, 1-5pm Sun; 🖳all city centre) and **Tamp & Stitch** (Unit 3, Scarlet Row, Essex St W; ⊙10am-6pm Mon-Sat; 🖳all city centre). Take a load off and enjoy a nice coffee.

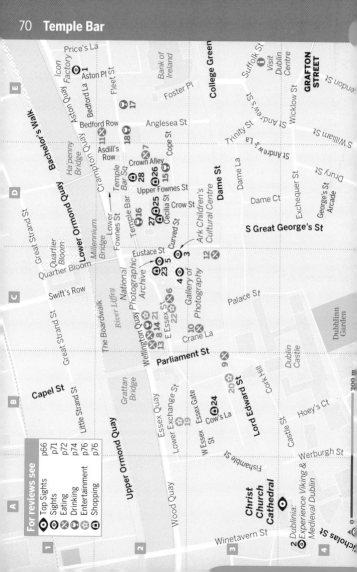

Sights

Dublin Musical Pub Crawl

WALKING

The story of Irish traditional music and its influence on contemporary styles is explained and demonstrated by two expert musicians in a number of Temple Bar pubs over 2½ hours. Tours meet upstairs in the Oliver St John Gogarty pub (see 17 ❓ Map p70, E2) and are highly recommended. (📞01-478 0193; www.discoverdublin.ie; 58-59 Fleet St; adult/student €14/12; ⏰7.30pm daily Apr-Oct, 7.30pm Thu-Sat Nov-Mar; 🚌all city centre)

Icon Factory

ARTS CENTRE

1 ◎ Map p70, E1

This fantastic artists collective in the heart of Temple Bar hosts exhibitions on Ireland's cultural heritage. You'll find colourful, unique souvenirs celebrating the very best in Irish music and literature and every sale goes towards the artists themselves. Take a stroll around their Icon Walk outside and get better acquainted with Irish playwrights, rock stars, sporting heroes and actors. (📞086 202 4533; www.iconfactorydublin.ie; 3 Aston Pl; admission free; ⏰11am-6pm; 🚌all city centre)

Dublinia: Experience Viking & Medieval Dublin MUSEUM

2 ◉ Map p70, A4

A must for the kids, the old Synod Hall, added to Christ Church Cathedral (p104) during its late 19th-century restoration, is home to the seemingly perennial Dublinia, a lively and kitschy attempt to bring Viking and medieval Dublin to life. Models, streetscapes and somewhat old-fashioned interactive displays do a fairly decent job of it, at least for kids. (☎01-679 4611; www.dublinia.ie; Christ Church Pl; adult/student/child €9.50/8.50/6, with Christchurch Cathedral €14.50/12/7.50; ◷10am-5.30pm Mar-Sep, to 4.30pm Oct-Feb; ☒50, 50A, 56A from Aston Quay, 54, 54A from Burgh Quay)

Ark Children's Cultural Centre CULTURAL CENTRE

3 ◉ Map p70, C2

Aimed at youngsters between the ages of three and 14, the Ark is a cultural centre that runs a range of age-specific programs, talks and interactive experiences to stimulate participants' interest in science, the environment and the arts. The centre also has an open-air stage for summer events. (www.ark.ie; 11a Eustace St; ☒all city centre)

Gallery of Photography GALLERY

4 ◉ Map p70, C2

This small gallery devoted to the photograph is set in an airy three-level space overlooking Meeting House Sq. It features a constantly changing menu of local and international work, as well as photography classes. The downstairs shop is well stocked with all manner of photographic tomes and manuals. (www.galleryofphotography.ie; Meeting House Sq; admission free; ◷11am-6pm Mon-Sat, 1-6pm Sun; ☒all city centre)

National Photographic Archive MUSEUM

5 ◉ Map p70, C2

The archive of photographs taken from the mid-19th century onward are part of the collection of the National Library, and so are open by appointment only and only with a reader's ticket, which can be obtained from the main branch (p59). (www.nli.ie; Meeting House Sq; admission free; ◷10am-1pm Tue-Thu, plus 2.30-4.30pm Wed; ☒all city centre)

Eating

Bunsen BURGERS €

6 ✖ Map p70, C2

The tag line says Straight Up Burgers, but Bunsen serves only the tastiest lumps of prime beef cooked to perfection and served between two halves of a homemade bap. Want fries? You've a choice between skinny, chunky or sweet potato. Order the double at your peril. There are two other branches: on **Wexford St** (36 Wexford St; ☒all city centre) and S Anne St (p40). (www.bunsen.ie; 22 Essex St E; burgers €7-10; ◷noon-9.30pm Mon-Wed, noon-10.30pm Thu-Sat, 1-9.30pm Sun; ☒all city centre)

Klaw
SEAFOOD €

7 🍴 Map p70, D2

There's nothing sophisticated about this crabshack-style place except the food: Irish oysters served naked, dressed or torched; Lambay Island crab claws served with a yuzu aioli; or half a lobster. Whatever you go for it's all delicious; the 'shucknsuck' oyster happy hour is a terrific deal with all oysters €1.50. (www.klaw.ie; 5a Crown Alley; mains €8-15; ⏰noon-10pm Mon-Wed & Sun, to 11pm Thu-Sat; 🚌all city centre)

Bison Bar & BBQ
BARBECUE €

8 🍴 Map p70, C2

Beer, whiskey sours and finger-lickingly good Texas-style barbecue – served on throwaway plates along with tasty sides such as slaw or mac 'n' cheese – is the fare at this boisterous restaurant. The cowboy theme is taken to the limit with the saddle chairs (yes, actual saddles); this is a place to eat, drink and be merry. (📞086 056 3144; www.bisonbar.ie; 11 Wellington Quay; mains €14-17; ⏰noon-9pm; 🚌all city centre)

Queen of Tarts
CAFE €

9 🍴 Map p70, B3

This cute little cake shop does a fine line in tarts, meringues, crumbles, cookies and brownies, not to mention a decent breakfast: the smoked bacon and leek potato cakes with eggs and cherry tomatoes are excellent. There's another, bigger, branch around the corner on **Cow's Lane** (3-4 Cow's Lane;

Understand
Ha'Penny Bridge

Dublin's most famous (and most photographed) bridge is officially called the Liffey Bridge, but everyone knows it by the name derived from the toll pedestrians were once charged to cross it. It was built in 1816 to replace a ferry service that operated here, and the charge was levied to recoup the £3000 building cost – a fortune at the time. The south bank's mooring point for the ferry was called Bagnio Slip (at the northern end of what is now Fownes St) – 'bagnio' is a term for a brothel.

🚌all city centre). (📞01-670 7499; www.queenoftarts.ie; 4 Cork Hill; mains €5-10; ⏰8am-8pm Mon-Fri, 8.30am-8pm Sat, 9am-7pm Sun; 🚌all city centre)

Skinflint
PIZZA €

10 🍴 Map p70, C3

Tables made out of old doors and kitchen paper as tablecloths...this is industrial-style pizza brought to you by the people who run Crackbird (p74) around the corner. The pizzas – all with girls' names like Viv, Breda and Philomena – are all super-thin and rectangular, and they use Irish rather than Type 00 Italian flour. The result is OK. (www.joburger.ie; 19 Crane Lane; pizzas €9-15; ⏰noon-10pm Tue-Thu, to 10.30pm Fri & Sat, noon-9pm Sun-Mon; 🚌all city centre)

Banyi Japanese Dining

JAPANESE €€

11 🍴 Map p70, E2

This compact restaurant in the heart of Temple Bar has arguably the best Japanese cuisine in Dublin. The rolls are divine, and the sushi as good as any you'll eat at twice the price. If you don't fancy raw fish, the classic Japanese main courses are excellent, as are the lunchtime bento boxes. Dinner reservations are advised, particularly at weekends. (📞01-675 0669; www.banyi japanesedining.com; 3-4 Bedford Row; lunch bento €11, small/large sushi platter €15/27; ⏱noon-11pm; 🖥all city centre)

Crackbird

FAST FOOD €€

12 🍴 Map p70, C3

It's a trendy version of fried chicken in a bucket, but it's oh so tasty. Choose between a half or full portion (half is enough for most humans) and add some sides – potato salad, chipotle baked beans, couscous or carrot and

---

☑ Top Tip

Sleep Elsewhere

Unless you're in for a no-holds-barred, knees-up weekend and don't care too much about sleeping, don't overnight in Temple Bar – hotel rooms are generally more cramped and noisier here than elsewhere. Temple Bar's central location and the city's size mean you can get in and out of here with relative ease.

---

cranberry salad – for extra flavour and variety. (www.joburger.ie; 60 Dame St; half/full roast chicken €12.50/22; ⏱noon-10pm Mon-Wed, to 11pm Thu-Sat, to 9pm Sun; 🛜; 🖥all city centre)

Cleaver East

MODERN IRISH €€

13 🍴 Map p70, C2

Michelin-starred chef Oliver Dunne has brought his cooking chops to bear in Cleaver East, where the decor (think New York brasserie but with cleavers everywhere) is as macho as some of the mains – feast on a succulent 'pornburger' or the excellent mains – the #roadtotipp is 200g of ground Hereford prime rib in a Jameson whiskey glaze. Very tasty. (📞01-531 3500; www.cleavereast.ie; Clarence, 6-8 Wellington Quay; tasting plates €10-14, main courses €17-26; ⏱12.30-3pm Fri-Sun & 5.30-10.30pm daily; 🖥all city centre)

Drinking

Liquor Rooms

COCKTAIL BAR

14 🍺 Map p70, C2

A subterranean cocktail bar decorated in the manner of a Prohibition-era speakeasy. There's lots of rooms – and room – for hip lounge cats to sprawl and imbibe both atmosphere and a well-made cocktail. There's dancing in the Boom Room, classy cocktails in the Blind Tiger Room and art-deco elegance in the Mayflower Room. (📞087 339 3688; www.theliquorrooms.com; 5 Wellington Quay; ⏱5pm-2am Mon-Thu & Sun, to 3am Fri & Sat; 🖥all city centre)

Vintage Cocktail Club BAR

15 Map p70, D2

The atmosphere behind this inconspicuous, unlit doorway initialled with the letters 'VCC' is that of a Vegas rat pack hang-out or a '60s-style London members' club. It's so popular you'll need to book for one of the 2½-hour evening sittings, which is plenty of time to sample some of the excellent cocktails and finger food. (www.vintagecocktailclub.com; Crown Alley; ⊙5pm-1.30am Mon-Fri, 12.30pm-1.30am Sat & Sun; ⊒all city centre)

Temple Bar BAR

16 Map p70, D2

The most photographed pub facade in Dublin, perhaps the world, the Temple Bar (aka Flannery's) is smack bang in the middle of the tourist precinct and is usually chock-a-block with visitors. It's good craic, though, and presses all the right buttons, with traditional musicians, a buzzy atmosphere and even a beer garden. (☎01-677 3807; 48 Temple Bar; ⊙10.30am-1.30am Mon-Wed, to 2.30am Thu-Sat, 11.30am-1am Sun; ⊒all city centre)

Oliver St John Gogarty PUB

17 Map p70, E2

You won't see too many Dubs ordering drinks in this bar, which is almost entirely given over to tourists who come for the carefully manufactured slice of authentic traditionalism...and the knee-slappin', toe-tappin' sessions that run throughout the day. The kitchen serves up Irish cuisine of questionable

Smock Alley Theatre (p76)

quality. (www.gogartys.ie; 58-59 Fleet St; ⊙10.30am-11.30pm Mon-Thu, to 12.30am Fri & Sat, noon-11pm Sun; ⊒all city centre)

Auld Dubliner PUB

18 Map p70, E2

Predominantly patronised by tourists, 'the Auld Foreigner', as locals have dubbed it, has a carefully manicured 'old world' charm that has been preserved after a couple of renovations. It's a reliable place for a singsong and a laugh, as long as you don't mind taking 15 minutes to get to and from the jax (toilets). (☎01-677 0527; www.aulddubliner.ie; 24-25 Temple Bar; ⊙10.30am-11.30pm Mon & Tue, 10.30am-2.30am Wed-Sat, 12.30-11pm Sun; ⊒all city centre)

Entertainment

Smock Alley Theatre
THEATRE

19 ⭐ Map p70, B2

One of the city's most diverse theatres is hidden in this beautifully restored 17th-century building. It boasts a diverse program of events (expect anything from opera to murder mystery nights, puppet shows and Shakespeare) and many events also come with a dinner option. (☑01-677 0014; www.smockalley.com; 6-7 Exchange St)

Mother
CLUB

20 ⭐ Map p70, B3

The best club night in the city is ostensibly a gay night, but it does not discriminate: clubbers of every sexual orientation come for the sensational DJs – mostly local but occasionally from abroad – who throw down a mixed bag of disco, modern synth-pop and other danceable styles. (www.twitter.com/motherdublin; Copper Alley, Exchange St; €10; ☺11pm-3.30am Sat; 📖all city centre)

Workman's Club
LIVE MUSIC

21 ⭐ Map p70, C2

A 300-capacity venue and bar in the former working-men's club of Dublin. The emphasis is on keeping away from the mainstream, which means everything from singer-songwriters to electronic cabaret. When the live music at the Workman's Club (Twitter: @WorkmansClubs) is over, DJs take

to the stage, playing rockabilly, hip hop, indie, house and more. (☑01-670 6692; www.theworkmansclub.com; 10 Wellington Quay; free-€20; ☺5pm-3am; 📖all city centre)

Project Arts Centre
THEATRE

22 ⭐ Map p70, C2

The city's most interesting venue for challenging new work – be it drama, dance, live art or film. Three separate spaces allow for maximum versatility. You never know what to expect, which makes it all that more fun: we've seen some awful rubbish here, but we've also seen some of the best shows in town. (☑1850 260 027; www.projectartscentre.ie; 39 Essex St E; ☺45min before showtime; 📖all city centre)

Shopping

Temple Bar Food Market
MARKET

23 🔒 Map p70, C2

From sushi to salsa, this is the city's best open-air food market; pick, prod and poke your way through the organic foods of the world with a compact stroll through gourmet lane. There are tastes of everywhere, from cured Spanish chorizo and paellas to Irish farmhouse cheeses, via handmade chocolates, freshly made crêpes, homemade jams and freshly squeezed juices. (www.facebook.com/TempleBarFood Market; Meeting House Sq; ☺10am-5pm Sat; 📖all city centre)

Gutter Bookshop BOOKS

24 🔒 Map p70, B3

Taking its name from Oscar Wilde's famous line from *Lady Windermere's Fan* – 'We are all in the gutter, but some of us are looking at the stars' – this fabulous place is flying the flag for the downtrodden independent bookshop, stocking a mix of new novels, children's books, travel literature and other assorted titles. (📞01-679 9206; www.gutterbookshop.com; Cow's Lane; ⊙10am-6.30pm Mon-Wed, Fri & Sat, to 7pm Thu, 11am-6pm Sun; 🖥all city centre)

Claddagh Records MUSIC

25 🔒 Map p70, D2

An excellent collection of good-quality traditional and folk music is the mainstay at this centrally located record shop. The profoundly knowledgable staff should be able to locate even the most elusive recording for you. There's also a decent selection of world music. There's another branch on Westmoreland St; you can also shop online. (📞01-677 0262; www.claddaghrecords.com; 2 Cecilia St; ⊙10am-6pm Mon-Sat, noon-6pm Sun; 🖥all city centre)

Lucy's Lounge VINTAGE

26 🔒 Map p70, D2

Go through the upstairs boutique and you'll find a staircase to an Aladdin's basement of vintage goodies. You can easily while away an hour or two here before re-emerging triumphant with something unique to brighten up your wardrobe. Looking for something specific? The super-friendly staff know where everything is hiding. (📞01-677 4779; www.lucysloungevintage.com; 11 Lower Fownes St; ⊙noon-6pm; 🖥all city centre)

Siopaella Design Exchange VINTAGE

27 🔒 Map p70, D2

A secondhand shop like no other in Dublin: you're as likely to find a vintage Chanel bag priced at €3000 as you are a beautiful preloved shirt for €5. You can exchange clothes for cash, or clothes for other clothes. One of the best shopping experiences in town. There's another branch on Wicklow St. (www.siopaella.com; 25 Temple Lane S; ⊙noon-6pm Mon-Wed, Fri & Sat, to 7pm Thu; 🖥all city centre)

Temple Bar Book Market MARKET

28 🔒 Map p70, D2

Bad secondhand potboilers, sci-fi, picture books and other assorted titles invite you to rummage about on weekend afternoons. If you look hard enough, you're bound to find something worthwhile. (Temple Bar Sq; ⊙11am-6pm Sat & Sun; 🖥all city centre)

Explore

Kilmainham & the Liberties

Dublin's oldest and most traditional neighbourhoods have a handful of tourist big hitters, not least the Guinness Storehouse, the city's most popular museum. There's also a whiskey distillery, a medieval cathedral and, further west, the country's premier modern-art museum and a Victorian prison that played a central role in Irish history.

The Sights in a Day

☀️ Take your time in **St Patrick's Cathedral** (p82), but be sure to go round the corner and pop into **Marsh's Library** (p88, pictured left). As you make your way through the Liberties, stop by the **Teeling Distillery** (p88) to take its enthusiastic tour. Finish your morning in the **Guinness Storehouse** (p80), Dublin's number-one tourist attraction.

☀️ Head further west again and explore the collection at the **Irish Museum of Modern Art** (p88) and take the tour of **Kilmainham Gaol** (p84) – but be prepared to wait patiently. If you do have to wait, head back into the gardens at IMMA or make your way towards the river to the **War Memorial Gardens** (p89).

🌙 A gig at **Vicar Street** (p93), a drink in **Fallon's** (p91) in the Liberties or, if you're still around Kilmainham, an evening in the **Old Royal Oak** (p91) – any of these will be a wonderful and authentic experience.

👁️ Top Sights

Guinness Storehouse (p80)

St Patrick's Cathedral (p82)

Kilmainham Gaol (p84)

💙 Best of Dublin

Sights

Irish Museum of Modern Art (p88)

Marsh's Library (p88)

Eating

Fumbally (p89)

Union8 (p91)

Legit Coffee Co (p90)

1837 Bar & Brasserie (p90)

Getting There

🚌 **Bus** Nos 50, 50A and 56A from Aston Quay and the 55 and 54A serve the cathedrals and the Liberties; for Kilmainham (including Irish Museum of Modern Art) use bus 51, 51D, 51X, 69, 78 or 79 from Aston Quay or the Luas to Heuston, from which it's a short walk.

🚶 **Walk** It's a 1.5km walk to the Guinness Storehouse from the city centre; about 3km to IMMA and Kilmainham Gaol.

Top Sights
Guinness Storehouse

More than any beer produced anywhere in the world, Guinness has transcended its own brand and is not just the best-known symbol of the city but a substance with near spiritual qualities, according to its legions of devotees the world over. A visit to the factory museum where it's made is therefore something of a pilgrimage for many of its fans.

Map p86, E3

www.guinness-storehouse.com

St James's Gate, Sth Market St

adult/child €18/16.50, Connoisseur Experience €48

9.30am-5pm Sep-Jun, to 6pm Jul & Aug

21A, 51B, 78, 78A, 123 from Fleet St, James's

A Drink of Guinness

This is the only true purpose of your visit: everything else is just window-dressing. Savour the moment the cold, bitter liquid passes your lips for the first time, for *this* is what Guinness at its very best tastes like.

Pouring the Perfect Pint

The 4th floor is all about learning how to pour the perfect pint – courtesy of expert instruction from the Guinness ambassadors, who will reward your best effort with a certificate of expertise. And give you the pint to drink.

The Connoisseur Experience

Real aficionados can opt for the Connoisseur Experience, where you sample the four different kinds of Guinness – Draught, Original, Foreign Extra Stout and Black Lager – while hearing their story from your designated bartender.

Gravity Bar

The last stop in the visit – and where you're given a glass of the black gold – is the 7th-floor Gravity Bar, a circular room with floor-to-ceiling windows that give 360-degree views of the city. OK, so it's not New York City, but you can see the whole skyline.

1837 Bar & Brasserie

Sitting one floor below the Gravity Bar and blessed with the same views of the city is this surprisingly good lunchtime spot (p90) that would be worth checking out as a standalone restaurant, never mind one in a museum.

☑ Top Tips

▶ Prebooking your tickets online will save you money.

▶ Try to visit midweek to avoid the worst of the crowds.

▶ Book ahead for the Connoisseur and Guinness Ambassador Experiences.

✖ Take a Break

In the shadow of the museum is the Legit Coffee Co (p90), which does good sandwiches and even better coffee. For something a little stronger, Arthur's (p91) is a terrific little pub.

Top Sights
St Patrick's Cathedral

Situated on the very spot that St Paddy supposedly rolled up his sleeves and dunked the heathen Irish into a well and thereby gave them a fair to middling shot at salvation, St Patrick's Cathedral is one of Dublin's earliest Christian sites and a most hallowed chunk of real estate.

⊙ Map p86, H3

www.stpatrickscathedral.ie

St Patrick's Close; adult/child €6.50/free

⊙ 9.30am-5pm Mon-Fri, 9am-6pm Sat, 9-10.30am & 12.30-2.30pm Sun

🚌 50, 50A, 56A from Aston Quay, 54, 54A from Burgh Quay

St Patrick's Park and Cathedral

Swift's Tomb

Entering the cathedral from the southwestern porch you come almost immediately, on your right, to the graves of Swift and his longtime companion Esther Johnson, aka Stella. On the wall nearby are Swift's own (self-praising) Latin epitaphs to the two of them, and a bust of Swift.

Boyle Monument

You can't miss the huge Boyle Monument, erected in 1632 by Richard Boyle, Earl of Cork. A figure in a niche at the bottom left of the monument is the earl's son Robert, the noted scientist who discovered Boyle's Law, which determined that the pressure and volume of a gas have an inverse relationship at a constant temperature.

'Peace Door'

The door in the north transept has a hole through which the earl of Kildare in 1472 extended his hand as a peace offering to the earl of Ormond, who was on the other side. Thankfully, the two earls made up and the expression 'to chance your arm' was born.

A Sung Service

Attend a sung Mass for the best atmosphere – at 11.15am on Sundays throughout the year, or at 9am Monday to Friday during school term only.

☑ **Top Tips**

▶ Advance tickets are not valid on Sundays between 10.45am and 12.30pm and between 2.45pm and 4.30pm.

▶ Last admission is 30 minutes before closing time.

✕ **Take a Break**

Cross Clanbrassil St and head for Fumbally (p89) for a sandwich or a hot bite. If you need something to fortify your spirits before or after your visit, Fallon's (p91) is one of Dublin's best pubs... and is conveniently only a short walk away.

Top Sights
Kilmainham Gaol

If you have *any* interest in Irish history, you must visit this infamous prison. It was the stage for many of the most tragic and heroic episodes in Ireland's recent past, and its list of inmates reads like a who's who of Irish nationalism. Solid and sombre, its walls absorbed the hardship of British occupation and recount it in whispers to visitors.

👁 Map p86, A3

📞 01-453 2037

www.kilmainhamgaol museum.ie; Inchicore Rd

adult/child €8/4

🕑 9.30am-6.45pm Jul & Aug, to 5.30pm rest of year

🚌 69, 79 from Aston Quay, 13, 40 from O'Connell St

East Wing
The prison's most distinctive and photogenic section is the east wing, built in 1862 and featuring 96 cells designed to keep the prisoners separate and in silence. Prison authorities forbade inmates from communicating with each other and encouraged them to contemplate their crimes and read the Bible.

Stone Breakers' Yard
Between 3 and 12 May 1916, the 14 leaders of the failed Easter Rising were executed in the yard, beginning with Patrick Pearse and ending with James Connolly, who was too injured to stand and was shot while strapped to a chair. Once news of their executions was released, the tide of public opinion began to turn in their favour – during the Rising it had been very much against the abortive attempt.

Asgard & Museum
Incongruously sitting outside in the yard is the *Asgard,* the ship that successfully ran the British blockade to deliver arms to nationalist forces in 1914. It belonged to, and was skippered by, Erskine Childers, father of the future president of Ireland. He was executed by Michael Collins' Free State army in 1922 for carrying a revolver, which had been a gift from Collins himself. There is also an outstanding museum dedicated to Irish nationalism and prison life.

☑ Top Tip
▶ Arrive early to avoid the usually long queues; try to get on the first tour of the day (tours can't be booked in advance).

✗ Take a Break
The Old Royal Oak (p91) is one of the city's most authentic traditional bars. For excellent contemporary Irish cuisine try Union8 (p91).

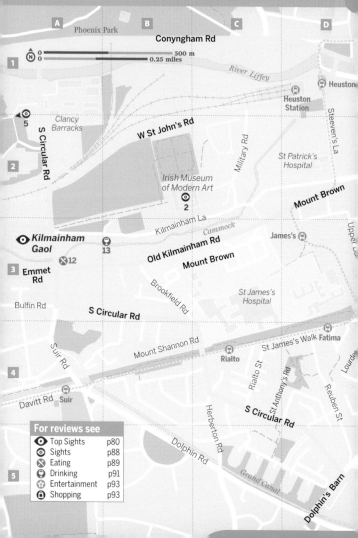

A **B** **C** **D**

Phoenix Park

Conyngham Rd

⬤ N
0   500 m
0   0.25 miles

River Liffey

1

⊙ 5

Clancy
Barracks

S Circular Rd

W St John's Rd

Heuston

Heuston
Station

Steeven's La

Military Rd

St Patrick's
Hospital

Mount Brown

2

Irish Museum
of Modern Art

2

Kilmainham La

Cammock

James's

Upper

◉ **Kilmainham
Gaol**

🚉 13

Old Kilmainham Rd

Mount Brown

3

Emmet
Rd

✕ 12

Brookfield Rd

Mount Brown

St James's
Hospital

Bulfin Rd

S Circular Rd

Mount Shannon Rd

Rialto

St James's Walk Fatima

Suir Rd

Rialto St

St Anthony's Rd

Lourdes

4

Davitt Rd   Suir

Herberton Rd

S Circular Rd

Reuben St

Dolphin Rd

Grand Canal

Dolphin's Barn

For reviews see
⊙	Top Sights	p80
⊙	Sights	p88
✕	Eating	p89
🍺	Drinking	p91
☆	Entertainment	p93
🔒	Shopping	p93

5

E Museum

Benburb St

Blackhall Pl

F Queen St

Bow St

Mary's La

G Lower Church St

Four
Courts

E Arran St

H

1

olfe Tone Quay

Ellis Quay

Smithfield

Four Courts

James Joyce
Bridge

Arran Quay

Upper Ormond Quay

Usher's Quay

Watling St

Bridgefoot St

Merchant's
Quay

Essex Quay

Winetavern St

Lord
Edward St

Castle St

17

St Augustine St

Oliver Bond St

Lower
Bridge St

High St

Nicholas St

Bride St

2

11

orse
ms
tillery

James's St

15

Thomas St

10

18

Swift's Al

Catherine St

Francis St

Golden La

St Patrick's
Cathedral

3

Guinness
Storehouse

Rainsford St

Bellevue

7

Robert St

S Earl St

8

Meath St

Meath Pl

Marrowbone La

Pimlico

S John St

The Coombe

Ardee St

14

Patrick St

Marsh's
Library

3

Upper Kevin St

Cork St

Newmarket
Teeling
Distillery

1 19

Mill St

S New Row

Blackpitts

6

New St

Long La

New Bride St

4

Dolphin's Barn

Fingal St

S Brown St

O'Curry Rd

St Thomas Rd

Clarence Mangan Rd

St Teresa's Gardens

Donore Ave

Susan Tce

9

Upper Clanbrassil St

Emorville Ave

Emor St

Arnott St

5

OLPHIN'S
BARN

Circular Rd

Dufferin Ave

Ingram Rd

16

S Circular Rd

Sights

Teeling Distillery
DISTILLERY

1 ◎ Map p86, G4

The first new distillery in Dublin for 125 years, Teeling only began production in 2015 and it will be several years before any of the distillate can be called whiskey. In the meantime, you can explore the visitor centre and taste (and buy) whiskeys from the family's other distillery on the Cooley Peninsula. (www.teelingwhiskey.com; 13-17 Newmarket; tours €15-30; ⊙9.30am-5.30pm Mon-Fri; ▣27, 77A & 151 from city centre)

Irish Museum of Modern Art
MUSEUM

2 ◎ Map p86, B2

Ireland's most important collection of modern and contemporary Irish and international art is housed in the elegant, airy expanse of the Royal Hospital Kilmainham, designed by Sir William Robinson and built between 1684 and 1687 as a retirement home for soldiers. It fulfilled this role until 1928, after which it languished for nearly 50 years until a 1980s restoration saw it come back to life as this wonderful repository of art. (IMMA; www.imma.ie; Military Rd; admission free; ⊙11.30am-5.30pm Tue-Fri, 10am-5.30pm Sat, noon-5.30pm Sun, tours 1.15pm Wed, 2.30pm Sat & Sun; ▣51, 51D, 51X, 69, 78, 79 from Aston Quay, ▣Heuston)

◯ Local Life
Garden Walks
The Italianate garden at the Irish Museum of Modern Art (p88) is beautiful for a gentle amble, but one of the city's best-kept open secrets is the War Memorial Gardens (p89) in Kilmainham, which runs along the Liffey.

Marsh's Library
LIBRARY

3 ◎ Map p86, H3

This magnificently preserved scholars' library, virtually unchanged in three centuries, is one of Dublin's most beautiful open secrets and an absolute highlight of any visit. Atop its ancient stairs are beautiful, dark-oak bookcases, each crammed with 25,000 books, manuscripts and maps dating back to the 15th century. (www.marsh library.ie; St Patrick's Close; adult/child €3/free; ⊙9.30am-5pm Mon & Wed-Fri, 10am-5pm Sat; ▣50, 50A, 56A from Aston Quay, 54, 54A from Burgh Quay)

Pearse Lyons Distillery
DISTILLERY

4 ◎ Map p86, E2

This boutique distillery opened in the former St James's Church in the summer of 2017, distilling small-batch, craft Irish whiskey. On the tour you will explore the distilling process and indulge in a range of Pearse Irish whiskies, including a blend, a sherry cask and a 12-year-old. (☎01-825 2244; www.pearselyonsdistillery.com; 121-122

War Memorial Gardens

James's St; guided tours €20; ⊒21A, 51B, 78, 78A, 123 from Fleet St)

War Memorial Gardens   PARK

5 ⊙ Map p86, A1

Hardly anyone ever ventures this far west, but they're missing a lovely bit of landscaping in the shape of the War Memorial Gardens – as pleasant a patch of greenery as any you'll find in the heart of the Georgian centre. Designed by Sir Edwin Lutyens, the memorial commemorates the 49,400 Irish soldiers who died during WWI – their names are inscribed in the two huge granite bookrooms that stand at one end. (www.heritageireland.ie; South Circular Rd, Islandbridge; admission free; ⊗8am-dusk

Mon-Fri, 10am-dusk Sat & Sun; ⊒69, 79 from Aston Quay, 13, 40 from O'Connell St)

Eating

Fumbally   CAFE €

6 ⊗ Map p86, H4

A bright, airy warehouse cafe that serves healthy breakfasts, salads and sandwiches – while the occasional guitarist strums away in the corner. Its Wednesday dinner (mains €16) is an organic, locally sourced exploration of the cuisines of the world that includes a single dish (and its vegetarian variant) served in a communal dining experience; advance bookings suggested. (☑01-529 8732;

Understand
Distillery Craze

The Liberties might be dominated by the world-famous Guinness brewery, but Dublin's most traditional neighbourhood is set to once again become a major centre for the distilling of whiskey. The Teeling Distillery opened up in 2015 after a hiatus of nearly 200 years: the original Teeling Distillery opened in 1782 around the corner on Marrowbone Lane and operated for 40 years. In 2017 the Liberties welcomed the Pearse Lyons Distillery, which began operations in the former St James's Church on James St. Pearse Lyons and his wife Deirdre own a brewery and distillery in Kentucky (as well as the giant animal nutrition company Alltech), but this new project is close to his heart as Lyons' own grandfather is buried in the church's graveyard. And finally (for now, at least) the Dublin Liberties Distillery is scheduled to open in 2018 in a former mill and tannery on Mill St. It seems whiskey is very much back.

www.thefumbally.ie; Fumbally Lane; mains €5-9.50; ⊘8am-5pm Tue-Fri, 10am-5pm Sat, plus 7-9.30pm Wed; 🚌49, 54A from city centre)

1837 Bar & Brasserie   BRASSERIE €

7 🍴 Map p86, E3

This lunchtime brasserie serves up tasty dishes, from really fresh oysters to an insanely good Guinness burger. The drinks menu features a range of Guinness variants such as West Indian porter. Highly recommended for lunch if you're visiting the museum. (☎01-471 4602; www.guinness-storehouse.com; Guinness Storehouse, St James's Gate; mains €9-14; ⊘noon-3pm; 🚌21A, 51B, 78, 78A, 123 from Fleet St, 🚋James's)

Legit Coffee Co   CAFE €

8 🍴 Map p86, F3

A rare trendy spot in the middle of one of Dublin's most traditional streets, Legit is full of stripped-down wood, speciality teas and strong espressos. A great spot to enjoy a toasted brioche or a filling sandwich. (www.legitcoffeeco.com; 1 Meath Mart, Meath St; mains €4-8; ⊘7.30am-5pm Mon-Fri, 9.30am-5pm Sat; 🚋James's)

Gaillot et Gray   PIZZA €

9 🍴 Map p86, G5

Mon dieu, a French pizzeria? Gilles Gaillot and his wife Emma Gray have combined the forces of Emmental cheese and pizza (biscuit-thin sourdough bases) to create this delicious hybrid. It doesn't taste like classic Italian pizza, which is precisely the point. And it works. It also operates as a bakery. (☎01-454 7781; 59 Lower Clanbrassil St; pizzas €8-9; ⊘8am-10pm Tue-Sat; 🚌49, 54A from city centre)

Dublin Cookie Company
BAKERY €

10 🍽️ Map p86, F2

Artisanal cookies by Jenny and Elaine, made fresh all day right in front of you. It's always experimenting with new and exciting flavours, and offers strong, aromatic coffee and chocolate or cookie-flavoured milk. (☎01-473 6566; www.thedublincookieco.com; 29 Thomas St; cookies from €1; ⏰8am-5.30pm Mon-Fri, 10am-4pm Sat; 🚌13, 69 from city centre)

Leo Burdock's
FISH & CHIPS €

11 🍽️ Map p86, H2

The fresh cod and chips served these days in Dublin's most famous fish 'n' chip shop is no better than that found in most other chippers, but the deep-fried fumes of Burdock's reputation still count for something, judging by the longish queues for a 'Dubliner's caviar'. (2 Werburgh St; cod & chips €9.25; ⏰noon-2am Mon-Fri, to midnight Sat & Sun; 🚌all city centre)

Union8
MODERN IRISH €€

12 🍽️ Map p86, A3

A hub for the local community of Dublin 8, this terrific spot serves tasty breakfasts and contemporary Irish cuisine (beautifully presented fish dishes, succulent lamb and the like) for lunch and dinner. (☎01-677 8707; www.union8.ie; 740 South Circular Rd; mains €18-27; ⏰9am-9pm Sun-Tue, to 9.30pm Wed, to 10pm Thu-Sat; 🚌69, 79 from Aston Quay, 13, 40 from O'Connell St)

Drinking

Old Royal Oak
PUB

13 🚇 Map p86, B3

Locals are fiercely protective of this gorgeous traditional pub, which opened in 1845 to serve the patrons and staff of the Royal Hospital (now the Irish Museum of Modern Art). The clientele has changed, but everything else has remained the same, which makes this one of the nicest pubs in the city in which to enjoy a few pints. (11 Kilmainham Lane; ⏰10.30am-11.30pm Mon-Thu, to 12.30am Fri & Sat, noon-11pm Sun; 🚌68, 79 from city centre)

Fallon's
PUB

14 🚇 Map p86, G3

A fabulously old-fashioned bar that has been serving a great pint of Guinness since the end of the 17th century. Prize-fighter Dan Donnelly, the only boxer ever to be knighted, was head bartender here in 1818. A local's local. (☎01-454 2801; 129 The Coombe; ⏰10.30am-11.30pm Mon-Thu, to 12.30am Fri & Sat, noon-11pm Sun; 🚌123, 206, 51B from city centre)

Arthur's
PUB

15 🚇 Map p86, E2

Given its location, Arthur's could easily be a cheesy tourist trap, and plenty of Guinness Storehouse (p80) visitors do pass through the doors tempted by another taste of the black stuff. Instead it's a friendly, cosy bar with a menu full of good comfort food. Best visited in

Understand

A Sketch of Dublin's History

Dublin's modern Irish name, Baile Átha Claith, means 'Town of the Hurdle Ford', in reference to the original Celtic settlement on the Liffey's northern bank. There is absolutely no visible evidence that the Iron Age Celts ever arrived here – but they did, around 700 BC.

Even the three 12th-century behemoths of the Norman occupation – Dublin Castle, and Christ Church and St Patrick's Cathedrals owe more to Victorian home improvements than they do to their original era.

To get a tangible sense of Dublin's history, fast-forward to the middle of the 18th century, when the city's gentry decided that the squalid medieval burg they lived in wasn't quite the gleaming metropolis they deserved, and set about redesigning the whole place, to create Georgian Dublin.

The scaffolding had scarcely come down on the refurbishments when the Act of Union in 1801 caused Dublin to lose its 'second city of the Empire' appeal and descend into a kind of ghost-town squalor.

Dublin escaped the worst effects of the Potato Famine (1845–51), but the government's failure to properly address the disaster fuelled the fires of anti-British sentiment and rebellion. This culminated in an ill-planned and disastrous revolt at Easter of 1916, which laid waste to much of the city centre and resulted in the leaders' execution in the grounds of Kilmainham Gaol. The tide turned firmly in favour of full-blown independence, which was achieved after a war of sorts that lasted from 1920 to 1921.

A newly independent Ireland moved cautiously and conservatively through the decades until the 1960s, when the winds of liberal change began to grow. They blew stronger in the 1990s with the unparalleled prosperity of the Celtic Tiger, which lasted until the global financial crisis of 2008.

The resulting recession saw a collapse in property prices and a general air of despondency. The corner was finally turned by 2015 – the same year the Marriage Equality referendum was passed – but as the decade's end looms into view the city is facing a major housing crisis caused by high rents and limited stock.

the winter so you get the full benefit of the roaring fireplace and soft candle-light. (📞01-402 0914; www.arthurspub.ie; 28 Thomas St; 🕙noon-11.30pm Mon-Thu, 11am-12.30am Fri & Sat, 11am-11pm Sun; 🚌21A, 51B, 78, 78A, 123 from Fleet St, 🚊James's)

MVP
BAR

16 🚇 Map p86, G5

A small and friendly bar just off the beaten path that is home to potent and inventive cocktails. The menu is pure comfort food: baked and roast potatoes in all varieties. (📞01-558 2158; www.mvpdublin.com; 29 Upper Clanbrassil St; 🕙4-11.30pm Mon-Thu, to 12.30am Fri & Sat, to 11pm Sun; 🚌49, 54A, 77X from city centre)

Brazen Head
PUB

17 🚇 Map p86, G2

Reputedly Dublin's oldest pub, the Brazen Head has been serving thirsty patrons since 1198. The clientele consists of foreign-language students, tourists and some grizzly auld locals. (📞01-679 5186; www.brazenhead.com; 20 Lower Bridge St; 🕙10am-midnight Mon-Thu, 10am-12.30am Fri & Sat, 11am-midnight Sun; 🚌51B, 78A, 123 from city centre)

Entertainment

Vicar Street
LIVE MUSIC

18 ⭐ Map p86, G2

Vicar Street is a midsized venue with a capacity of around 1000, spread be-tween the table-serviced group-seating

✅ Top Tip

Shop Local

Some of the most interesting – and wackiest – shopping is done along Francis St in the Liberties, the home of antiquarians and, in recent years, art dealers of every hue. Although you mightn't fancy transporting the hand luggage, you can have that original Edwardian fireplace you've always wanted, shipped to you by the shop.

downstairs and a theatre-style balcony. It offers a varied program of perform-ers, from comedians to soul, jazz, folk and world music. (📞01-454 5533; www.vicarstreet.com; 58-59 Thomas St; tickets €25-60; 🕙7pm-midnight; 🚌13, 49, 54A, 56A from city centre)

Shopping

Dublin Food Co-op
MARKET

19 🔒 Map p86, G4

From dog food to detergent, every-thing in this member-owned co-op is organic and/or ecofriendly. Thursday has a limited selection of local and imported fair-trade products, but Saturday is when it's all on display – Dubliners from all over drop in for their responsible weekly shop. There's an on-the-premises baker and even baby-changing facilities. (www.dublinfood.coop; 12 Newmarket; 🕙10am-7pm Wed & Fri, to 8pm Thu, 9.30am-5pm Sat, 11am-5pm Sun; 🚌49, 54A, 77X from city centre)

Local Life
Wander the Wilds of Phoenix Park

Getting There

🚌 Nos 25, 26, 46A, 66/66A/66B, 67, 69 from city centre

🚃 Luas Red Line to Heuston Station

The hugely impressive 709 hectares that comprise Phoenix Park are not just a magnificent playground for all kinds of sport from running to polo, but are also home to the president of Ireland, the American ambassador and a shy herd of fallow deer. It is also where you'll find Europe's oldest zoo. How's that for a place to stretch your legs?

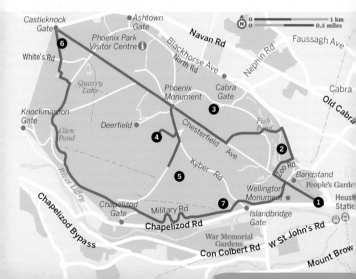

1 **Parkgate St Entrance**

Chesterfield Ave runs northwest through the **park** (www.phoenixpark. ie; admission free; ⏱24hr; 🚌10 from O'Connell St, 25, 26 from Middle Abbey St) to the Castleknock Gate. The 63m-high **Wellington Monument** obelisk was completed in 1861; nearby is the **People's Garden**, dating from 1864, and the **bandstand** in the Hollow.

2 **A Lion's Roar**

The 28-hectare **Dublin Zoo** (www. dublinzoo.ie; adult/child/family €17.50/13/49; ⏱9.30am-6pm Mar-Sep, to dusk Oct-Feb; 🚌10 from O'Connell St, 25, 26 from Middle Abbey St) opened its doors in 1831, making it one of the oldest in the world. It's been hugely developed, but its lion-breeding program dates back to 1857 – among its offspring is the lion that roars at the start of MGM films.

3 **The Presidential Pile**

If the 1751 Palladian mansion **Áras an Uachtaráin** (www.president.ie; admission free; ⏱guided tours hourly 10.30am-3.30pm Sat; 🚌10 from O'Connell St, 25, 26 from Middle Abbey St), the official residence of the Irish president, seems familiar, it's because it was James Hoban's inspiration for the White House. Take the free one-hour tour.

4 **A Cross Fit for a Pope**

Across Chesterfield Ave – and easily visible from the road – is the massive **Papal Cross** (🚌10 from O'Connell St, 25, 26 from Middle Abbey St), which marks the site where Pope John Paul II preached

to 1.25 million people in 1979. In the centre of the park, the Phoenix Monument, erected by Lord Chesterfield in 1747, looks so unlike a phoenix that it's often referred to as the Eagle Monument.

5 **Fifteen Acres**

This huge expanse of greenery south of the cross – where you're most likely to see the deer –is actually much bigger than 15 acres. At weekends, the pitches fill with soccer teams. On the other side of the cross is the old chief secretary's lodge, Deerfield, now the official residence of the US ambassador.

6 **Out to Farmleigh...**

Towards the Castleknock Gate is this fine Georgian-Victorian pile (📞01-815 5900; www.farmleigh.ie; Castleknock; admission free; ⏱10am-5pm Sat & Sun, guided tours hourly 10.15am-4.15pm; 🚌37 from city centre) designed by James Gandon. Only the ground floor, with a fantastic library and glass conservatory, is on view, but the pleasure gardens with lake, and walled and Japanese gardens are delightful for a stroll.

7 **...And Back into the City**

Take the side road around the southern perimeter. Back towards the Parkgate St entrance is the **Magazine Fort** (1801; see www. phoenixpark.ie for tours). It provided target practice during the 1916 Easter Rising, and was raided by the IRA in 1940, when the entire ammunition reserve of the Irish army was nabbed.

Explore

North of the Liffey

Grittier than its more genteel southside counterpart, the area immediately north of the River Liffey offers a fascinating mix of 18th-century grandeur, traditional city life and the multicultural melting pot that is contemporary Dublin. Beyond its widest, most elegant boulevard you'll find art museums and whiskey museums, bustling markets and some of the best ethnic eateries in town.

The Sights in a Day

☀ Saunter up O'Connell St, Dublin's grandest boulevard, past the **General Post Office** (p102, pictured left) – be sure to take a look inside – and toward Parnell Sq and the **Dublin City Gallery – Hugh Lane** (p98), which is well worth a couple of hours.

☀ Take the Luas light rail west and get off at Museum. Devote the remainder of the afternoon to the collection of the decorative arts and history section of the **National Museum** (p102) at Collins Barracks. It's a decent walk back to the city centre, but it'll give you a chance to appreciate the city's fine Georgian heritage up close via the **Four Courts** (p102) and **Henrietta Street** (p103).

☽ For that special meal, book a table at **Chapter One** (p106), which conveniently does a pre-theatre option so that you can head around the corner to take in a show at the **Gate Theatre** (p109).

◉ Top Sight

Dublin City Gallery – the Hugh Lane (p98)

💜 Best of Dublin

Modern Irish Cuisine
Chapter One (p106)

Fish Shop (p105)

Oxmantown (p104)

L Mulligan Grocer (p106)

Drinking
Cobblestone (p106)

Walshe's (p107)

Confession Box (p107)

Getting There

🚌 **Bus** All city centre buses stop on O'Connell St or the nearby quays. City buses serve Glasnevin and Croke Park, while national bus services, operated by Bus Eireann, arrive and depart from the Busáras depot on Store St.

🚋 **Tram** The Luas runs east to west parallel to the Liffey from The Point to Heuston Station.

🚆 **Train** The DART runs from Connolly Station northeast to Clontarf Rd, which is handy for the Casino at Marino. Mainline trains for the north and northwest go from Connolly Station.

Top Sights
Dublin City Gallery – the Hugh Lane

Whatever reputation Dublin may have as a repository of top-class art is in large part due to the collection at this magnificent gallery, home to Impressionist masterpieces, the best of modern Irish work from 1950 onward, and the actual studio of Francis Bacon.

👁 Map p100, F1

📞 01-222 5550, www. hughlane.ie

22 N Parnell Sq; free

🕙 9.45am-6pm Tue-Thu, to 5pm Fri & Sat, 11am-5pm Sun

🚌 7, 11, 13, 16, 38, 40, 46A, 123 from city centre

7 Reece Mews Francis Bacon Studio (photograph © The Estate of Francis Bacon. All rights reserved, DACS)

Francis Bacon Studio

The gallery's most popular exhibit is the Francis Bacon Studio, which was painstakingly moved, in all its shambolic mess, from 7 Reece Mews, South Kensington, London, where the Dublin-born artist (1909–92) lived for 31 years. The display features some 80,000 items madly strewn about the place, including slashed canvases and the last painting he was working on.

The Hugh Lane Bequest

The collection (known as the Hugh Lane Bequest 1917) was split in a complicated 1959 settlement that sees the eight masterpieces divided into two groups and alternated between Dublin and London every six years. The paintings currently on show (until 2021) are *Les Parapluies* (The Umbrellas) by Auguste Renoir, *Portrait of Eva Gonzales* by Edouard Manet, *Jour d'Été* (Summer's Day) by Berthe Morisot and *View of Louveciennes* by Camille Pissarro.

Sean Scully Gallery

The ground-floor gallery is dedicated to seven abstract paintings by Irish-born Sean Scully, probably Ireland's most famous living painter. Elsewhere in the new wing is work by other contemporary Irish artists including Dorothy Cross, Brian Maguire and Norah McGuinness.

The Eve of St Agnes

Just by the main reception desk is the Stained Glass gallery, whose highlight is Harry Clarke's wonderful *The Eve of St Agnes* (1924). His masterpiece is made up of 22 separate panels, each a depiction of a stanza of John Keats' eponymous poem about the doomed love between Madeline and Porphyro, who cannot meet because their families are sworn enemies.

☑ Top Tip

The gallery has developed a decent app and a growing online catalogue of its collection, which allows you to search by artist and view their work before (or after) your visit.

✗ Take a Break

You can round off a satisfying visit with lunch in the superb **cafe** (☎01-874 1903; mains €7-13) in the basement, before making a stop in the well-stocked **gift shop**.

Ｎ
0 _____ 500 m
0 _____ 0.25 miles

St Brendan's Hospital

For reviews see

⊙ Top Sights	p98
◉ Sights	p102
⊗ Eating	p104
⊕ Drinking	p106
★ Entertainment	p109
⊕ Shopping	p109

Philbsborough Rd

Prussia St

Aughrim St

Constitution Hill

Prebend St

Lower Grangegorman

Kirwan St

Manor Pl

Manor St

Morning Star Ave

Arbour Hill Cemetery

N Brunswick St

N King St

⊗13

⊕17 N King St

15
⊕

SMITHFIELD

Arbour Hill

National Museum of Ireland – Decorative Arts & History
⊙
1

Blackhall Pl

Queen St

Smithfield

Friary Ave

Bow St

2
◉
Old Jameson Distillery

May La

Lower Church St

Beresford St

Mary's L

Cuckoo

Benburb St

Hendrick St

Museum

⊗12

10
⊗

Wolfe Tone Quay

James Joyce Bridge

Smithfield

N Phoenix St Hammond La

Four Courts

Greek St

Four Courts

Arran Quay

Father Mathew Bridge

4
Four Courts ◉
Inns Quay

O'Don

Watling St

Island St

Bonham St

Bridgefoot St

Usher's Quay

Merchant's Quay

Ros...
Brid...

E

Fontenoy St

estern Way

F

N Frederick St

Great Denmark St

G

N Great George's St

Hill St

H

Grenville St

Upper Gardiner St

1

Mountjoy St

St Mary's Tce

Upper Dorset St

Upper Dominick St

Henrietta St

rrietta reet 5

Granby Row

Granby La

Dublin
City Gallery –
Hugh Lane 6

Dublin Writers
Museum

N Rutland Pl

W Rutland Pl

E Parnell Sq

Parnell St

Bolton St

Henrietta Pl

King's Inns St

Lower Dominick St

Dominick Pl

Dominick St

Dominick La

W Parnell Sq

Parnell
Sq 21

Cathal Brugha St

2

College of
Technology

Loftus La

Parnell St

Green St

ttle Britain St

Capel St

Wolfe Tone St

Jervis St

Chapel La

Parnell St

Upper O'Connell St

Dublin
Bus

Moore La

23

Moore St

Henry Pl

9

Cathedral St

N Earl St

16

Marlborough St

Talbot St

Earl Pl

Lower O'Connell St

3

Mary St

Lower Jervis St

Mary St

HenrySt

General Post Office

N Prince's St

3

Sackville Pl

Lower Abbey St

E Arran St

Little Mary St

8

St Mary's

Upper Abbey St

Jervis

Lower Jervis La

22

Middle Abbey St

Lotts Row

Abbey St

20

Harbour Ct

Eden
Quay

Mary's Abbey

18

Little Strand St

Great Strand St

19

14 11

Lower Liffey St

Bachelor's Walk

Ha'penny Bridge

Aston Quay

O'Connell
Bridge

Rosie
Hackett
Bridge

D'Olier St

Hawkins St

pper Ormond Quay

Grattan Bridge

River Liffey

od Quay Essex Quay

Essex Gate

Wellington Quay

Parliament St

Lower Ormond Quay

Millennium
Bridge

E Essex St

Eustace St

Temple Bar

Crow St

Temple La

Anglesea St

TEMPLE
BAR

Bank
of Ireland

Westmoreland St

Fleet St

College St

College Green

5

Dame St

Sights

National Museum of Ireland – Decorative Arts & History
MUSEUM

1 ◎ Map p100, A4

Once the world's largest military barracks, this splendid early neoclassical grey-stone building on the Liffey's northern banks was completed in 1704 according to the design of Thomas Burgh (he of Trinity College's Old Library). It is now home to the Decorative Arts & History collection of the National Museum of Ireland, with a range of superb permanent exhibits ranging from a history of the **Easter Rising** to the work of iconic Irish designer **Eileen Gray** (1878–1976). (www.museum.ie; Benburb St; admission free; ◎10am-5pm Tue-Sat, 2-5pm Sun; ◻25, 66, 67, 90 from city centre, ◾Museum)

Old Jameson Distillery
MUSEUM

2 ◎ Map p100, C4

Smithfield's biggest draw is devoted to *uisce beatha* (ish-kuh ba-ha, 'the water of life'); that's Irish for whiskey. To its more serious devotees, that is precisely what whiskey is, although they may be put off by the slickness of this museum (occupying part of the old distillery that stopped production in 1971), which shepherds visitors through a compulsory tour of the re-created factory (the tasting at the end is a lot of fun) and into the ubiquitous gift shop. (www.jamesonwhiskey.com; Bow St; adult/student/child €18/15/9, masterclasses €55; ◎10am-5pm Mon-Sat, 10.30am-5pm Sun; ◻25, 66, 67, 90 from city centre, ◾Smithfield)

General Post Office
HISTORIC BUILDING

3 ◎ Map p100, G3

It's not just the country's main post office, or an eye-catching neoclassical building: the General Post Office is at the heart of Ireland's struggle for independence. The GPO served as command HQ for the rebels during the Easter Rising of 1916 and as a result has become the focal point for all kinds of protests, parades and remembrances, as well as home to an interactive visitor centre. (☎01-705 7000; www.anpost.ie; Lower O'Connell St; ◎8am-8pm Mon-Sat; ◻all city centre, ◾Abbey)

Four Courts
HISTORIC BUILDING

4 ◎ Map p100, D5

This masterpiece by James Gandon (1743–1823) is a mammoth complex stretching 130m along Inns Quay, as fine an example of Georgian public architecture as there is in Dublin. Despite the construction of a brand-new criminal courts building further west along the Liffey, the Four Courts is still the enduring symbol of Irish law going about its daily business. Visitors are allowed to wander through the building, but not to enter courts or other restricted areas. (☎01-886 8000; Inns Quay; admission free; ◎9am-5pm Mon-Fri; ◻25, 66, 67, 90 from city centre, ◾Four Courts)

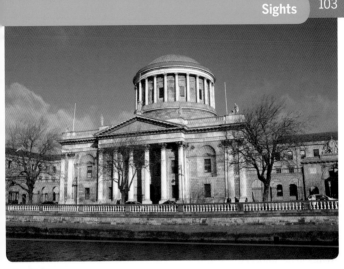

Four Courts

Henrietta Street STREET

5 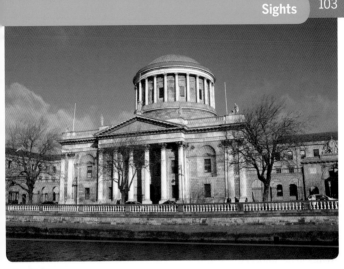 Map p100, E2

Henrietta St dates from the 1720s and was the first project of Dublin's pre-eminent Georgian developer, Luke Gardiner. It was designed as an enclave of prestigious addresses (Gardiner himself lived at No 10), and remained one of Dublin's most fashionable streets until the Act of Union (1801). It's a wonderful insight into the evolution of Georgian residential architecture, and features mansions of varying size and style. (☐ 25, 25A, 37, 38, 39, 66, 67, 90, 134 from city centre, ☐ Four Courts)

Dublin Writers Museum MUSEUM

6 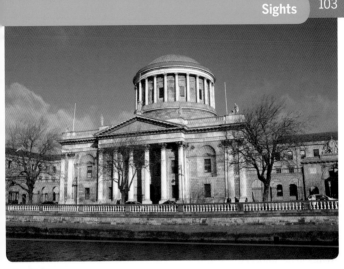 Map p100, G1

Memorabilia aplenty and lots of literary ephemera line the walls and display cabinets of this elegant museum devoted to preserving the city's rich literary tradition up to 1970. The building, comprising two 18th-century houses, is worth exploring on its own; Dublin stuccodore Michael Stapleton decorated the upstairs gallery. However, the curious decision to omit living writers limits its appeal – no account at all is given to contemporary authors, who would arguably be more popular with today's readers. (www. writersmuseum.com; 18 N Parnell Sq; adult/

Local Life

Stoneybatter Life

Just north of Collins Barracks, Stoneybatter is a traditional working-class neighbourhood given a hip makeover by college students and immigrants looking for affordable rents. L Mulligan Grocer (p106) does terrific contemporary Irish grub and craft beers, while nearby Walshe's (p107) is an aspic-soaked boozer that's not changed a jot in a century – and although it has a clutch of old regulars, none are quite so old as to have borne witness to the burials of the leaders of the Easter Rising in the nearby **Arbour Hill Cemetery** (☑01-821 3021; www.heritageireland.ie; Arbour Hill; admission free; ☺8am-4pm Mon-Fri, 11am-4pm Sat, 9.30am-4pm Sun; ☒25, 25A, 37, 38, 39, 66, 67, 90, 134 from city centre, ☒Museum).

child €8/5; ☺9.45am-4.45pm Mon-Sat, 11am-4.30pm Sun; ☒3, 7, 10, 11, 13, 16, 19, 46A, 123 from city centre)

Eating

Oxmantown   CAFE €

8 ☒ Map p100, E4

Delicious breakfasts and excellent sandwiches make this cafe one of the standout places for daytime eating on the north side of the Liffey. Locally baked bread, coffee supplied by Cloud Picker (Dublin's only microroastery) and meats sourced from Irish farms are the ingredients, but it's the way it's all put together that makes it so worthwhile. (www.oxmantown.com; 16 Mary's Abbey, City Markets; sandwiches €5.50; ☺7.30am-4pm Mon-Fri; ☒Four Courts, Jervis)

M&L   CHINESE €

9 ☒ Map p100, H3

Beyond the plain frontage and the cheap-looking decor is Dublin's best Chinese restaurant...by some distance. It's usually full of Chinese people, who come for the authentic Szechuan-style cuisine – spicier than Cantonese and with none of the concessions usually made to Western palates. (☑01-874 8038; www.mlchineserestaurant.com; 13/14 Cathedral St; mains €9-13; ☺11.30am-10pm Mon-Sat, noon-10pm Sun; ☒all city centre)

Fish Shop   SEAFOOD €€

10 ☒ Map p100, B4

The menu changes daily at this tiny restaurant to reflect what's fresh, but you'll have to trust them: your only choice is a four-course or tasting menu. One day you might fancy line-caught mackerel with a green sauce, another day slip sole with caper butter. Maybe the best seafood restaurant in town. (☑01-430 8594; www.fish-shop.ie; 6 Queen St; 4-course/tasting menu €39/55; ☺noon-2.30pm & 5-10pm Wed-Fri, 5-10pm Tue & Sat; ☒25, 25A, 66, 67 from city centre, ☒Smithfield)

Yarn   PIZZA €€

11 ☒ Map p100, G4

With a 1st-floor terrace view of the Ha'Penny Bridge, this might be the city's coolest pizza joint. Add that it serves excellent drinks (pizza and Aperol, anyone?) and its credentials are rock solid. Oh, and the pizza – thin base, pomodoro San Marzano and delicious mozzarella – is delicious. It's the sister restaurant to the **Woollen Mills** (www.thewoollenmills.com; 42 Lower Ormond Quay; sandwiches €10-11, mains €18-27; ⏱9am-11pm Mon-Fri, 9am-4pm & 5-11pm Sat, noon-4pm & 5-10.30pm Sun; 🚌all city centre) – hence the name. (www.theyarnpizza.com; 37 Lower Liffey St; pizzas €9-14; ⏱5-10pm; 🚌all city centre)

Fish & Chip Shop   FISH & CHIPS €€

12 🍴 Map p100, B4

A classic fish-and-chip shop with a gourmet, sit-down twist – not only is the fish the best you'll taste in battered form, but you'll wash it down with a fine wine from their carefully selected list. It's the original

Dublin Writers Museum (p103)

Fish Shop that moved from Queen St, where its fancier sister restaurant is now installed. (📞01-557 1473; www.fish-shop.ie; 76 Benburb St; mains

---

Understand

Da Nort'soyid & the Southsyde

It is commonly assumed that the southside is totally posh and the northside is a derelict slum – it makes the jokes easier to crack and the prejudices easier to maintain. But the truth is a little more complex. The 'southside' generally refers to Dublin 4 and the fancy suburbs immediately west and south – conveniently ignoring the traditionally working-class neighbourhoods in southwestern Dublin such as Bluebell and Tallaght. North Dublin is huge, but the northside tag is usually applied to the inner suburbs, where incomes are lower, accents are more pronouncedly Dublin and – most recently – the influx of foreign nationals is more in evidence.

€12.50-14.50; ⏱ noon-1pm Tue-Fri, 4-10pm Sat & Sun; 🚌 25, 25A, 66, 67 from city centre, 🚊 Museum)

L Mulligan Grocer   MODERN IRISH €€

13 🍴 Map p100, B3

It's a great traditional pub, but the main reason to come here is for the food, all sourced locally and made by expert hands. The menu includes slow-cooked free-range pork belly and herb-crumbed haddock, as well as a particularly tasty lamb burger. There are about a dozen craft beers on draught and as many again in a bottle. (📞 01-670 9889; www.lmulligangrocer.com; 18 Stoneybatter; mains €15-29; ⏱ 4-10pm Mon-Fri, 12.30-10pm Sat & Sun; 🚌 25, 25A, 66, 67 from city centre, 🚊 Museum)

Winding Stair   MODERN IRISH €€

14 🍴 Map p100, G4

In a beautiful Georgian building that once housed the city's most beloved bookshop – the ground floor still

is one (p109) – the Winding Stair's conversion to elegant restaurant has been faultless. The wonderful Irish menu (creamy fish pie, bacon and organic cabbage, steamed mussels, and Irish farmyard cheeses) coupled with an excellent wine list makes for a memorable meal. (📞 01-873 7320; www.winding-stair.com; 40 Lower Ormond Quay; 2-course lunch €22, mains €22-28; ⏱ noon-5pm & 5.30-10.30pm; 🚌 all city centre)

Chapter One   MODERN IRISH €€€

Flawless haute cuisine and a relaxed, welcoming atmosphere make this Michelin-starred restaurant in the basement of the Dublin Writers Museum (see 6◎ Map p100, G1) our choice for best dinner experience in town. The food is French-inspired contemporary Irish, the menus change regularly and the service is top-notch. The three-course pre-theatre menu (€39.50) is great if you're going to the Gate (p109) around the corner. (📞 01-873 2266; www.chapteronerestaurant.com; 18 N Parnell Sq; 2-course lunch €32.50, 4-course dinner €75; ⏱ 12.30-2pm Tue-Fri, 7.30-10.30pm Tue-Sat; 🚌 3, 10, 11, 13, 16, 19, 22 from city centre)

Drinking

Cobblestone   PUB

15 🍺 Map p100, C3

It advertises itself as a 'drinking pub with a music problem', which is an apt description for this Smithfield stalwart

✓ Top Tip

Street Smart

By day, O'Connell St is a bustle of activity, with shoppers, hawkers, walkers and others going about their business. At night, however, it can be a different story, as alcohol and drugs can give the street an air of menace and, sadly, the odd spot of trouble, so you'll have to keep your wits about you.

– although the traditional music sessions that run throughout the week can hardly be described as problematic. Wednesday's Balaclava session (from 7.30pm) is for any musician who is learning an instrument, with musician Síomha Mulligan on hand to teach. (www.cobblestonepub.ie; N King St; ⏱4.30-11.30pm Mon-Thu, to 12.30am Fri & Sat, 1.30-11.30pm Sun; 🚇Smithfield)

Confession Box   PUB

16 🚇 Map p100, H3

This historic pub is popular with tourists and locals alike. Run by some of the friendliest bar staff you're likely to meet, it's also a good spot to brush up on your local history: the pub was a favourite spot of Michael Collins, one of the leaders in the fight for Irish independence. (📞01-874 7339; www.c11407968.wixsite.com/ryan; 88 Marlborough St; ⏱11am-11pm Mon-Fri, 10am-midnight Sat & Sun; 🚇Abbey)

Walshe's   PUB

17 🚇 Map p100, B3

If the snug is free, a drink in Walshe's is about as pure a traditional experience as you'll have in any pub in the city; if it isn't, you'll have to make do with the old-fashioned bar, where the friendly staff and brilliant clientele (a mix of locals and trendsetting imports) are a treat. A proper Dublin pub. (6 Stoneybatter; ⏱10.30am-11.30pm Mon-Thu, to 12.30am Fri & Sat, noon-11pm Sun; 🚌25, 25A, 66, 67 from city centre, 🚇Museum)

Winding Stair

Pantibar   GAY & LESBIAN

18 🚇 Map p100, F4

A raucous, fun gay bar owned by Rory O'Neill, aka Panti, star of 2015's acclaimed documentary *The Queen of Ireland,* about the struggle for equality that climaxes in the historic marriage referendum of May 2015. The bar has since become a place of LGBTQ pilgrimage – and no-holds-barred enjoyment. (www.pantibar.com; 7-8 Capel St; ⏱5-11.30pm Mon, Wed & Sun, to 2am Tue, to 2.30am Thu-Sat; 🚇all city centre)

Grand Social   BAR

19 🚇 Map p100, G4

This multipurpose venue hosts club nights, comedy and live-music gigs,

Understand

James Joyce

Dublin's greatest literary son is James Joyce, author of *Ulysses*, the greatest novel of the 20th century – although we're yet to meet five people who've actually finished it. Still, Dubliners are immensely proud of the writer once castigated as a literary pornographer by locals and luminaries alike – even George Bernard Shaw dismissed him as vulgar.

Born in the south Dublin suburb of Rathgar in 1882, the young Joyce grew up north of the Liffey before fleeing town in 1904 with the love of his life, Nora Barnacle. He spent most of the next 10 years in Trieste, where he wrote prolifically but struggled to get published. His career was further hampered by recurrent eye problems and he had 25 operations for glaucoma, cataracts and other conditions.

The first major prose he finally had published was *Dubliners* (1914), a collection of short stories set in the city, including the three stories he had written in Ireland. Publishers began to take notice and his autobiographical *A Portrait of the Artist as a Young Man* (1916) followed. In 1918 the US magazine *Little Review* started to publish extracts from *Ulysses* but notoriety was already pursuing his epic work and the censors prevented publication of further episodes after 1920.

Passing through Paris on a rare visit to Dublin, he was persuaded by Ezra Pound to stay a while in the French capital. What he intended to be a brief visit turned into a 20-year stay. It was a good move for the struggling writer for, in 1922, he met Sylvia Beach of the Paris bookshop Shakespeare & Co, who finally managed to put *Ulysses* (1922) into print. The publicity from its earlier censorship ensured instant success.

Buoyed by the success of the inventive *Ulysses*, Joyce went for broke with *Finnegans Wake* (1939), 'set' in the dreamscape of a Dublin publican. Perhaps not one to read at the airport, the book is a daunting and often obscure tome about eternal recurrence. It is even more complex than *Ulysses* and took the author 17 years to write.

In 1940 WWII drove the Joyce family back to Zürich, Switzerland, where the author died the following year.

and is a decent bar for a drink. It's spread across three floors, each of which has a different theme: the Parlour downstairs is a cosy, old-fashioned bar; the midlevel Ballroom is where the dancing is; and the upstairs Loft hosts a variety of events. (📞01-874 0076; www.thegrandsocial.ie; 35 Lower Liffey St; ⏰4pm-2.30am Thu-Sat, to 11.30pm Sun-Wed; 🚇all city centre, 🚇Jervis)

Entertainment

Abbey Theatre
THEATRE

20 ⭐ Map p100, H4

Ireland's national theatre was founded by WB Yeats in 1904 and was a central player in the development of a consciously native cultural identity. In 2017 it appointed Neil Murray and Graham McLaren of the National Theatre of Scotland as its new directors, and they have promised an exciting new program that will fuse traditional and contemporary fare. (📞01-878 7222; www.abbeytheatre.ie; Lower Abbey St; 🚇all city centre, 🚇Abbey)

Gate Theatre
THEATRE

21 ⭐ Map p100, G2

The city's most elegant theatre, housed in a late 18th-century building, features a generally unflappable repertory of classic Irish, American and European plays. It is the only theatre in town where you might see established international movie stars work on their credibility with a theatre run. (📞01-874 4045; www.gatetheatre.ie; 1 Cavendish Row; ⏰performances 7.30pm Mon-Sat, 2.30pm Wed; 🚇all city centre)

Shopping

Winding Stair
BOOKS

This handsome old bookshop is in a ground-floor room when once upon a time it occupied the whole building, which is now given over to an excellent restaurant (see 14 ❌ Map p100, G4) of the same name. Smaller selection, but still some excellent quality new and old-book perusals. (📞01-872 6576; www.winding-stair.com; 40 Lower Ormond Quay; ⏰10am-6pm Mon-Wed & Fri, to 7pm Thu & Sat, noon-6pm Sun; 🚇all city centre)

Arnott's
DEPARTMENT STORE

22 🔒 Map p100, G4

This is our favourite of Dublin's department stores. It stocks virtually everything, from garden furniture to high fashion, and it's all relatively affordable. (📞01-805 0400; www.arnotts.ie; 12 Henry St; ⏰10am-6pm Mon-Wed, Fri & Sat, to 7pm Thu, noon-6pm Sun; 🚇all city centre)

Moore Street Market
MARKET

23 🔒 Map p100, G3

A shadow of its vibrant former self, this is the most traditional of Dublin street markets. You can get fruit, fish and flowers, while other vendors hawk cheap cigarettes and other products. (Moore St; ⏰8am-4pm Mon-Sat; 🚇all city centre)

Explore

Docklands

The gleaming modern blocks of the Docklands were designed as the ultimate expression of the ambitions of the Celtic Tiger. The collapse of 2008 put a curb on those ambitions, but the city's recent revival has reinvigorated the area. A couple of architectural beauties – most notably a theatre designed by Daniel Libeskind – stand out among the modern apartment and office blocks.

The Sights in a Day

☀️ After you've photographed the **Custom House** (p115), take a close look at Rowan Gillespie's **Famine Memorial** (p115) just to the east. Then board the **Jeanie Johnston** (p116, pictured left) and imagine the real-life versions of the sculptures making their way across the Atlantic for a new life in the US.

☀️ Devote the afternoon to a spot of sightseeing: the Dockland bridges make a great photo op, as does the **Bord Gáis Energy Theatre** (p119) and the modern square in front of it. Grand Canal Dock is lined with cafes: pick one and while away the afternoon.

🌙 After dinner – **Juniors Deli & Cafe** (p117) or **Paulie's Pizza** (p117) – you've a choice between a big-ticket gig at the **3 Arena** (p119) or a concert at the **Bord Gáis Energy Theatre** (p119). In the event that neither has something on when you visit, a night in the pub – **John Mulligan's** (p117), for instance – will be more than enough consolation.

For a local's day exploring the Docklands' hidden heritage, see p112.

🔍 **Local Life**

The Docklands' Hidden Heritage (p112)

💜 **Best of Dublin**

Entertainment
3 Arena (p119)

Bord Gáis Energy Theatre (p119)

Architecture
Custom House (p115)

Convention Centre (p113)

Samuel Beckett Bridge (p113)

Grand Canal Square (p113)

Getting There

🚌 **Bus** The most convenient public transport option is the bus – Nos 1, 47, 56A and 77A go from Dame St to the edge of Grand Canal Sq. For the northside, bus 151 goes from Bachelor's Walk to the Docklands.

🚊 **Tram** The Luas Red Line terminus is at the Point Village.

🚆 **Train** The DART stops at Grand Canal Quay.

Local Life
The Docklands' Hidden Heritage

Bright and gleaming, the docklands may be the city's newest development – most of the buildings are barely 10 years old – but in between the shiny architectural boxes are bits of Dublin heritage, including links to the Easter Rising. Oh, and some nice bridges that will afford some pretty picture options.

1 **A Little Excise on Spencer Dock**

The docklands east of the Custom House are the hub of Dublin's financial services sector. Excise Walk, just past the Jeanie Johnston, is the perfect spot to start with a coffee, or something more substantial at **Eddie Rocket's** (☎01-524 0152; North Wall Quay; burgers €7-9; ⊙11.30am-10pm Sun-Thu, to 11pm Fri & Sat; 🚌Mayor Square – NCI) on the waterfront.

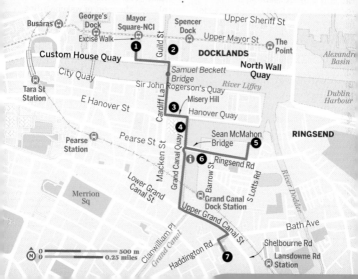

❷ Heritage & History

Explore the history of migration – and maybe your own heritage? – at the high-tech **EPIC Irish Emigration Museum** (Map p114, B2; ☎01-906 0861; www.epicchq.com; CHQ Bldg, Custom House Quay; adult/child €14/7; ⊙10am-6.45pm, last entrance 5pm; 🚉George's Dock) inside the CHQ building, where you'll also find the **Irish Family History Centre** (Map p114, B2; ☎01-671 0338; www.irishfamily historycentre.com; CHQ Bldg, Custom House Quay; €9.50, incl EPIC The Irish Emigration Museum €22; ⊙10am-5pm; 🚉George's Dock). Here you can get a personalised take on your Irish roots.

❸ Going to a Convention?

You can't miss Kevin Roche's eye-catching 2010 **Convention Centre** (Spencer Dock, North Wall Quay; ⊙closed to the public; 🚉Mayor Square – NCI), with its angled, glass-fronted atrium that has become one of the city's most distinctive buildings. Cross to the south side of the river via the **Samuel Beckett Bridge** (🚉Spencer Dock), which looks like a giant wishbone.

❹ From the Rooftop Marker Bar

Walk up Cardiff Lane and turn left onto the inappropriately named Misery Hill (neither miserable nor steep). On your left, directly facing the Bord Gáis Energy Theatre is the **Marker Hotel** (☎01-687 5100; www.themarker hoteldublin.com; Grand Canal Sq; r/ste from €350/520; P@🛜; 🚉Grand Canal Dock), whose rooftop bar is *the* trendy spot to have a drink.

❺ Grand Canal Square

From your elevated vantage point, you've a fine view of the **square** (Map p114, C3; 🚉Grand Canal Dock) below, which was designed by American landscape artist Martha Schwartz and opened in 2008. Its most distinctive feature is the red 'carpet' made of bright red, resin-glass paving covered with red, glowing, angled light sticks.

❻ Wakeboarding

Cross Sean McMahon Bridge and head to the eastern end of the dock, where you'll find the ramps and apparatus of **Wakedock** (☎01-664 3883; www.wakedock. ie; Grand Canal Dock; 30min tuition adult/ student €60/45; ⊙noon-8pm Tue-Fri, 10am-8pm Sat & Sun; 🚌1, 15A, 15B, 56A, 77A from city centre, 🚉Grand Canal Dock), which has popularised the sport of wakeboarding.

❼ Rising Links and Gleaming Towers

Backtrack to the boxlike building near Sean McMahon Bridge, the Waterways Visitor Centre. Facing it is the old Boland's Flour Mill, which most Dubliners think was the operational HQ for Eamon De Valera's IRA battalion during the Easter Rising...but it wasn't. The actual HQ was at Boland's Bakery, now occupied by the Treasury Building (to get here, walk left along Grand Canal Quay to the northwestern corner of Grand Canal St and Macken St). Climbing the side of the building is *Aspiration*, by Rowan Gillespie, who did the *Famine* Memorial on Custom House Quay.

A
B
C
D

1

Summerhill Pde

Diamond
Park

Portland Row

N Strand Rd

West Rd

Church Rd

St Mary's Rd

East Rd

East Wall

**EAST
WALL**

500 m
0.25 miles

Lower Sean MacDermot St

Railway St

Amiens St

Seville Pl

Royal Canal

Lower Gardiner St

Foley St

Talbot St

**Connolly
Station**

Sheriff St

Connolly

Commons St

Lower
Sheriff St

Docklands

Upper Sheriff St

2

Busáras

**George's
Dock**

**Mayor
Square - NCI**

Guild St

NORTH WALL

**The
Point**

Custom
House

Lower Major St

Upper Mayor St

Spencer
Dock

12

1 ⊙ **Famine**
Memorial

2 ⊙

4 ⊙

5 ⊙

⊙ **EPIC The Irish**
Emigration Museum

8

Irish Family
History Centre

3 ⊙ **Jeanie**
Johnston

Samuel
Beckett
Bridge

North Wall Quay

9 ⊗ ⊗

City Quay

River Liffey

Sir John Rogerson's Quay

Tara St
Station

Townsend St

E Lombard St

East Hanover St

Lime St

Cardiff La

Hanover Quay

3

Pearse St

Westland Row

Erne St
Lower

Grand Canal Docks

Trinity College

Pearse
Station

Erne St
Upper

Pearse St

11 ⊛

Nassau St

Fenian St

Lower Grand Canal St

Macken St

13 🔒

Ringsend Rd

Barrow St

S Lotts Rd

Bridge St

River Dodd

4

Kildare St

N Merrion Sq

Lower Mount St

Merrion
Square

S Merrion Sq

Grand Canal St

Upper Grand
Canal St

Grand Canal
Dock Station

Shelbourne
Park Greyhound
Stadium

St Stephen's
Green

7 ⊗

10 ⊗

6 ⊗

Bath Ave

Herbert Pl

Haddington Rd

Northumberland Rd

National
Print
Museum

Shelbourne Rd

Lansdowne Rd
Station

5

Mespil Rd

For reviews see

⊙ Sights	p115
⊗ Eating	p117
⊕ Drinking	p117
⊛ Entertainment	p119
🔒 Shopping	p119

Poolbeg Lighthouse (p116)

Sights

Custom House MUSEUM

1 🎯 Map p114, A2

Georgian genius James Gandon (1743–1823) announced his arrival on the Dublin scene with this magnificent building (1781–91), constructed just past Eden Quay at a wide stretch in the River Liffey. It's a colossal, neoclassical pile that stretches for 114m topped by a copper dome, beneath which the **visitor centre** (€1.50; ⏱10am-12.30pm Mon-Fri, 2-5pm Sat & Sun mid-Mar–Oct, closed Mon, Tue & Sat Nov–mid-Mar) features a small museum on Gandon and the history of the building. (Custom House Quay; ⏱9am-5pm Mon-Fri; 🚌all city centre)

Famine Memorial MEMORIAL

2 🎯 Map p114, A2

Just east of the Custom House (p115) is one of Dublin's most thought-provoking examples of public art: the set of life-size bronze figures (1997) by Rowan Gillespie known simply as *Famine*. Designed to commemorate the ravages of the Great Hunger (1845–51), their haunted, harrowed look testifies to a journey that was both hazardous and unwelcome. (Custom House Quay; 🚌all city centre)

Jeanie Johnston MUSEUM

3 Map p114, B3

One of the city's most original tourist attractions is an exact working replica of a 19th-century 'coffin ship', as the sailing boats that transported starving emigrants away from Ireland during the Famine were gruesomely known. A small on-board museum details the harrowing plight of a typical journey, which usually took around 47 days. (www.jeaniejohnston.ie; Custom House Quay; adult/student/child/family €10/9/5.50/25;

Local Life
Poolbeg Lighthouse

One of the city's most rewarding walks is a stroll along the Great South Wall to the **Poolbeg Lighthouse** (South Wall; ⏱24hr; 🚌1, 47, 56A, 77A, 84N from city centre), that red tower visible in the middle of Dublin Bay. The lighthouse dates from 1768, but it was redesigned and rebuilt in 1820. To get there, take the bus to Ringsend from the city centre, and then make your way past the power station to the start of the wall (it's about 1km). It's not an especially long walk out to the lighthouse – about 800m or so – but it will give you a stunning view of the bay and the city behind you, a view best enjoyed just before sunset on a summer's evening.

⏱tours hourly 10am-4pm Apr-Oct, 11am-3pm Nov-Mar; 🚌all city centre, 🚊George's Dock)

EPIC The Irish Emigration Museum MUSEUM

4 Map p114, B2

This is a high-tech, interactive exploration of emigration and its effect on Ireland and the 70 million or so people spread throughout the world who claim Irish ancestry. Start your visit with a 'passport' and proceed through 20 interactive – and occasionally moving – galleries examining why they left, where they went and how they maintained their relationship with their ancestral home. (📞01-906 0861; www.epicchq.com; CHQ Bldg, Custom House Quay; adult/child €14/7; ⏱10am-6.45pm, last entrance 5pm; 🚊George's Dock)

Irish Family History Centre CULTURAL CENTRE

5 Map p114, B2

Discover your family history with interactive screens where you can track your surname and centuries of Irish emigration. The ticket price also includes a 15-minute consultation with a genealogist. You can visit as part of the EPIC (p113) exhibition or buy a separate ticket. (📞01-671 0338; www.irishfamilyhistorycentre.com; CHQ Bldg, Custom House Quay; €9.50, incl EPIC The Irish Emigration Museum €22; ⏱10am-5pm; 🚊George's Dock)

Eating

Juniors Deli & Cafe   ITALIAN €€

6 🍴 Map p114, D4

Cramped and easily mistaken for any old cafe, Juniors is anything but ordinary. Designed to imitate a New York deli, the food (Italian-influenced, all locally sourced produce) is delicious, the atmosphere always buzzing (it's often hard to get a table) and the ethos top-notch, which is down to the two brothers who run the place. (📞01-664 3648; www.juniors.ie; 2 Bath Ave; mains €18-21; ⏰8.30am-2.30pm & 5.30-10pm Mon-Fri, 11am-3pm & 5.30-10.30pm Sat, 11am-3.30pm Sun; 🚌3 from city centre, 🚆Grand Canal Dock)

Paulie's Pizza   ITALIAN €€

7 🍴 Map p114, C4

At the heart of this lovely, occasionally boisterous restaurant is a Neapolitan pizza oven, used to create some of the best pizzas in town. Margheritas, *biancas* (no tomato sauce), calzoni and other Neapolitan specialities are the real treat, but there's also room for a classic New York slice and a few local creations. (www.juniors.ie; 58 Upper Grand Canal St; pizzas €12-18; ⏰6-10pm; 👶; 🚌3 from city centre, 🚆Grand Canal Dock)

Workshop Gastropub   MODERN IRISH €€

8 🍴 Map p114, A3

Take a traditional pub and introduce a chef with a vision: hey presto, you've

Top Tip

Eating & Drinking

Grand Canal Dock has a couple of decent spots for food, but even better ones are to be found southwest at the junction of Haddington Rd, Upper Grand Canal St and Bath Ave, where you'll find a handful of terrific restaurants and popular pubs.

got a gastropub (surprisingly one of the few in the city) serving burgers, *moules frites* (mussels served with French fries) and sandwiches, as well as a good range of salads. (Kennedy's; 📞01-677 0626; www.theworkshopgastropub.com; 10 George's Quay; mains lunch €7-9, dinner €10-24; ⏰noon-3pm Mon-Fri, to 4.45pm Sat & Sun; 👶; 🚌all city centre, 🚆Tara St)

Drinking

John Mulligan's   PUB

9 🍺 Map p114, A3

This brilliant old boozer is a cultural institution, established in 1782 and in this location since 1854. A drink (or more) here is like attending liquid services at a most sacred, secular shrine. John F Kennedy paid his respects in 1945, when he joined the cast of regulars that seems barely to have changed since. (www.mulligans.ie; 8 Poolbeg St; ⏰10.30am-11.30pm Mon-Thu, to 12.30am Fri & Sat, noon-11pm Sun; 🚌all city centre)

Understand

Literary Dublin

Dublin's storied past is covered by a wide range of history books, while the city's literary festivals are a great opportunity to meet Irish and international authors up close.

Books on Dublin History

Dublin: The Making of a Capital City (2014) David Dickson

Come Here to Me: Dublin's Other History (2013) Donal Fallon, Sam McGrath and Ciaran Murray

Dublin: A Cultural & Literary History (2005) Siobhán Kilfeather

Stones of Dublin: A History of Dublin in Ten Buildings (2014) Lisa Marie Griffith

A Short History of Dublin (2010) Richard Killeen

Book Festivals

International Literature Festival Dublin (☎01-969 5259; www.ilfdublin.com; ⏰May) The city's biggest literary event is a great showcase of local and international talent.

Dublin Book Festival (www.dublinbookfestival.com; ⏰mid-Nov) A three-day festival of literature with readings and talks.

Dalkey Book Festival (www.dalkeybookfestival.org; ⏰mid-Jun) A small festival with an impressive line-up.

Mountains to the Sea Dlr Book Festival (www.mountainstosea.ie; ⏰mid-Mar) The southside suburb of Dún Laoghaire gets literary.

Slattery's   PUB

10 🚇 Map p114, D4

A decent boozer that is a favourite with rugby fans who didn't get
tickets to the match – they congregate
around the TVs and ebb and flow
with each passage of the game. It's
also popular on Friday and Saturday
nights. (📞01-668 5481; www.slatterysd4.
ie; 62 Upper Grand Canal St; ⏰1-11.30pm
Mon-Thu, noon-12.30am Fri & Sat, noon-11pm
Sun; 🚌4, 7, 8, 120 from city centre)

Entertainment

Bord Gáis
Energy Theatre   THEATRE

11 ⭐ Map p114, C3

Forget the uninviting sponsored
name: Daniel Libeskind's masterful
design is a three-tiered, 2100-capacity
auditorium where you're as likely to be
entertained by the Bolshoi or a touring
state opera as you are to see *Disney
on Ice* or Barbra Streisand. It's a magnificent venue – designed for classical,
paid for by the classics. (📞01-677 7999;
www.grandcanaltheatre.ie; Grand Canal Sq;
🚊Grand Canal Dock)

3 Arena   LIVE MUSIC

12 ⭐ Map p114, D2

The premier indoor venue in the city
has a capacity of 23,000 and plays
host to the brightest touring stars in

Understand
Shopping Traditional

Traditional Irish products such as
crystal and knitwear remain popular choices, and you can increasingly find innovative modern takes
on the classics. But steer clear of
the mass-produced junk whose
joke value isn't worth the hassle of
carting it home on the plane: trust
us, there's no such thing as a genuine *shillelagh* (Irish fighting stick)
for sale anywhere in town.

the firmament. Radiohead, Bob Dylan
and Take That performed here in
2017. (📞01-819 8888; www.3arena.ie; East
Link Bridge, North Wall Quay; tickets €30-90;
⏰6.30-11pm; 🚊The Point)

Shopping

Design Tower   ARTS & CRAFTS

13 🔒 Map p114, C4

Housed in a 19th-century warehouse
that was Dublin's first iron-structured
building, this seven-storey design
centre houses studios for around 20
local craftspeople, producing everything from Celtic-inspired jewellery to
wall hangings and leather bags. Some
studios are open by appointment only;
check the website for details. (📞01-677
5655; www.thedesigntower.com; Pearse St;
⏰9am-5pm Mon-Fri; 🚊Grand Canal Dock)

Explore

The Southside

The neighbourhoods that border the southern bank of the Grand Canal are less about sights and more about the experience of affluent Dublin – dining, drinking and sporting occasions, both watching and taking part. These are the city's most desirable neighbourhoods to live in – especially Ballsbridge (pictured above), Donnybrook and Ranelagh.

The Sights in a Day

☀ The **National Print Museum** (p123), in a former barracks, is a fascinating insight into the history of print in Ireland - and there are lots of machines to examine up close. A spot of brunch in **Farmer Brown's** (p123) is always a good idea.

☀ If it's a pleasant day, stretch your legs in **Herbert Park** (p123), which has tennis courts, a bowling green and plenty of space for exercise, or just lying around. Just south of here is Ailesbury Road, aka 'Embassy Row' – a beautiful road with some of Dublin's most exclusive residences. This is where some of the 1% live.

☽ Hop on the Luas to Ranelagh and get some dinner at either **Kinara** (p124) or the **Butcher Grill** (p124) before getting a post-prandial pint or two at the **Taphouse** (p124), aka Russell's. If it's a nice summer's night you can sit on the balcony and watch village life go by.

 Best of Dublin

Eating

Farmer Brown's (p123)

Butcher Grill (p124)

Kinara (p124)

Chophouse (p124)

Entertainment

Aviva Stadium (p125)

Bowery (p125)

Royal Dublin Society Showground (p125)

Getting There

🚌 **Bus** From the city centre, take bus Nos 5, 7, 7A, 8, 45, 46 to Ballsbridge; for Donnybrook the 10A or 46; and for Rathmines Nos 14 or 15.

🚊 **Tram** The Luas green line serves Ranelagh from St Stephen's Green.

🚆 **Train** The DART serves Sandymount (for Bath Ave) and Lansdowne Road.

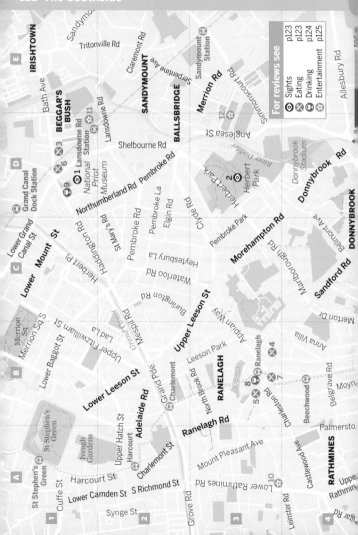

IRISHTOWN

Sandymount Rd

Tritonville Rd

Claremont Rd

Serpentine Ave

Bath Ave

BEGGAR'S
BUSH

Lansdowne Rd

Lansdowne Rd

Lansdowne Station

Shelbourne Rd

SANDYMOUNT

Sandymount Station

Merrion Rd

Simmonscourt Rd

BALLSBRIDGE

Anglesea St

Merrion Rd

Ailesbury Rd

National Print Museum

Northumberland Rd

Pembroke Rd

Pembroke Rd

St Mary's Rd

Haddington Rd

Herbert Pl

Lower Mount St

Grand Canal Dock Station

Lower Grand Canal St

Merrion Sq S

Merrion Sq

Lower Baggot St

Upper Fitzwilliam St

Grand Canal

Mespil Rd

Pembroke La

Elgin Rd

Clyde Rd

Pembroke Park

Herbert Park

River Dodder

Herbert Park

DONNYBROOK

Donnybrook Stadium

Donnybrook Rd

Morehampton Rd

Marlborough Rd

Sandford Rd

Belmont Ave

Merton Dr

Anna Villa

Waterloo Rd

Burlington Rd

Heytesbury La

Lad La

Upper Leeson St

Lower Leeson St

Adelaide Rd

Upper Hatch St

Charlemont

Grand Pde

Leeson Park

Appian Way

North Brook Rd

Leeson Park

RANELAGH

Ranelagh

Belgrave Rd

Beechwood

Moyn

St Stephen's Green

Cuffe St

Iveagh Gardens

Harcourt St

Lower Camden St

S Richmond St

Charlemont St

Charlemont

Harcourt

Ranelagh Rd

RANELAGH

Charleston Rd

Castlewood Ave

Palmersto

RATHMINES

Synge St

Grove Rd

Lower Rathmines Rd

Mount Pleasant Ave

Leinster Rd

Upper

Rathmin

ear Rd

Sights

National Print Museum   MUSEUM

1 Map p122, D1

You don't have to be into printing to enjoy this quirky little museum, where guided tours (11.30am daily and 2.30pm Monday, Tuesday, Thursday and Friday) are offered in a delightfully casual and compelling way. A video looks at the history of printing in Ireland and then you wander through the various (still working) antique presses amid the smell of ink and metal. (01-660 3770; www.nationalprintmuseum.ie; Haddington Rd, Garrison Chapel, Beggar's Bush; adult/concession €3.50/2; 9am-5pm Mon-Fri, 2-5pm Sat & Sun; 4, 7 from city centre, Grand Canal Dock, Lansdowne Rd)

Herbert Park   PARK

2 Map p122, D3

A gorgeous swath of green lawns, ponds and flower beds near the Royal Dublin Society Showground (p125). Sandwiched between prosperous Ballsbridge and Donnybrook, the park runs along the River Dodder. (Ballsbridge; dawn-dusk; 5, 7, 7A, 8, 45, 46, Sandymount, Lansdowne Rd)

Eating

Farmer Brown's   INTERNATIONAL €€

3 Map p122, D1

The hicky-chic decor and mismatched furniture won't be to

Royal Dublin Society Showground (p125)

everyone's liking, but there's no disagreement about the food, which makes this spot our choice for best brunch in Dublin. From healthy smashed avocado to a stunning Cuban pork sandwich, it has all your lazy breakfast needs covered. Very much worth the effort. There's another **branch** (086-046 8837; www.farmerbrowns.ie; 170 Lower Rathmines Rd; mains €10-26; 10am-10pm Mon-Sat, to 9pm Sun; 14, 15 from city centre) in Rathmines. (01-660 2326; www.farmerbrowns.ie; 25a Bath Ave; brunch €10-12, dinner €14-26; 11am-10pm Mon-Fri, 10am-10pm Sat & Sun; ; 7, 8 from city centre, Grand Canal Dock)

Butcher Grill

INTERNATIONAL €€

4 ✘ Map p122, B3

No surprise that this terrific spot specialises in meat, which is locally sourced and cooked to perfection in its wood-smoked grill. Dishes include barbecued baby back ribs and a superb *côte de boeuf* (rib steak) to share. Locals will also argue that the brunch is the best in the city. (☑01-498 1805; www.the butchergrill.ie; 92 Ranelagh Rd; mains €20-28; ⊙5.30-9.30pm Sun-Wed, to 10.30pm Thu-Sat, plus noon-3pm Sat & Sun; ☐Ranelagh)

Kinara

PAKISTANI €€

5 ✘ Map p122, B3

Connoisseurs of the various cuisines of South Asia can distinguish between Indian and Pakistani fare; this exceptional restaurant specialising in the latter will soon educate even the most inexperienced palate. Curries such as the *nehari gosht* (made with beef) are superb, as are fish dishes, including the *machali achari* (fillet of red snapper simmered with pickles). (☑01-406 0066; www.kinarakitchen.ie; 17 Ranelagh Rd; mains €19-30; ⊙5-11pm daily, plus noon-3pm Thu & Fri, 1-5pm Sun; ☐Ranelagh)

Local Life
Brilliant for Brunch
Gourmands from all over the city trek to the likes of Butcher Grill (p124) and Dillinger's (p124) in Ranelagh, and Farmer Brown's (p123) on Bath Ave for the relaxed weekend brunch.

Chophouse

GASTROPUB €€

6 ✘ Map p122, D1

This fine sprawling bar is a terrific gastropub where the focus is on juicy cuts of steak, but reluctant carnivores also have a choice of fish, chicken or lamb dishes. It does an excellent Sunday lunch – the slow-braised pork belly is delicious. It's a popular watering hole when there's a match on at the Aviva Stadium (p125). (☑01-660 2390; www.thechophouse.ie; 2 Shelbourne Rd; lunch €12-25, dinner €19-35; ⊙restaurant noon-2.30pm & 6-10pm Mon-Fri, 5-10pm Sat, 1-8pm Sun; ☐4, 7, 8, 120 from city centre)

Dillinger's

AMERICAN €€

7 ✘ Map p122, B3

This trendy American-style diner is small, so expect a wait if you want to go for the (excellent) weekend brunch. It's worth it just to taste the amazing things they can do with pulled pork, and if you're craving American-style pancakes, this is the place for you. (☑01-497 8010; www.dillingers.ie; 47 Ranelagh Rd; ⊙5.30-9.30pm Mon & Tue, to 10.30pm Wed & Thu, to 11pm Fri, 11am-4pm & 5.30-11pm Sat, 11am-4pm & 5.30-9.30pm Sun; ☐Ranelagh)

Drinking

Taphouse

BAR

8 ☐ Map p122, B3

Locals refer to it by its original name of Russell's, but that doesn't mean that the regulars aren't delighted with the spruce-up the new owners have brought to a village favourite. What they didn't change was the beloved balcony – the best spot to have a drink on a warm day. (☎01-491 3436; www.taphouse.ie; 60 Ranelagh Rd; ⏱12.30pm-12.30am Mon-Sat, to 11pm Sun; 🚊Ranelagh)

Beggar's Bush   PUB

9 ⓖ Map p122, D1

A staunch defender of the traditional pub aesthetic, Ryan's (as it's referred to by its older clientele) has adjusted to the modern age by adding an outside patio for good weather. Everything else, though, has remained the same, which is precisely why it's so popular with flat-capped pensioners and employees from nearby Google. (Jack Ryan's; 115 Haddington Rd; ⏱11am-11pm; 🚌4, 7, 8, 120 from city centre, 🚊Grand Canal Dock)

Entertainment

Bowery   LIVE MUSIC

10 ⓖ Map p122, A3

With its burnished wood, intricate chandeliers and ship-shaped stage, this music venue is one of the best-looking bars in the city. It features live performances every night of the week, from ska to disco to reggae, and upstairs is an excellent people-watching spot. (www.thebowery.ie; 196 Lower Rathmines Rd;

Fancy a Run?
Herbert Park (p123) is an excellent spot for a run and can be easily reached on foot from most city-centre hotels.

⏱5pm-midnight Sun-Thu, to 12.30am Fri & Sat; 🚌14, 65, 140)

Aviva Stadium   STADIUM

11 ⓖ Map p122, D1

Gleaming 50,000-capacity ground with an eye-catching curvilinear stand in the swanky neighbourhood of Donnybrook. Home to Irish rugby and football internationals. (☎01-238 2300; www.avivastadium.ie; 11-12 Lansdowne Rd; 🚊Lansdowne Rd)

Royal Dublin Society Showground   SPECTATOR SPORT

12 ⓖ Map p122, D3

This impressive, Victorian-era showground is used for various exhibitions throughout the year. The most important annual event here is the late-July **Dublin Horse Show**, which includes an international showjumping contest. Leinster rugby also plays its home matches in the 35,000-capacity arena. Ask at the tourist office for other events. (RDS Showground; ☎01-668 9878; Merrion Rd, Ballsbridge; 🚌7 from Trinity College)

The Best of
Dublin

Dublin's Best Walks

Dublin's Best...

Samuel Beckett Bridge and Convention Centre (p113)
TUZIMEK/SHUTTERSTOCK ©

Best Walks
Take a Walk on the North Side

🏃 The Walk

North of the river, the graceful avenue that is O'Connell St introduces visitors to what was once the city's most desirable neighbourhood. Georgian Dublin was born here, on Parnell and Mountjoy squares; it played a starring role in the nation's struggle for independence, as you'll see in the General Post Office; and it is still home to some of the best museums in town.

Start Mountjoy Sq

Finish St Michan's Church

Length 2.5km; two hours

✕ Take a Break

Oxmantown (p104) serves sandwiches on locally baked bread and Cloud Picker coffee, provided by Dublin's only microroastery.

YKKAAJ/SHUTTERSTOCK ©

Abbey Presbyterian Church

❶ St George's Church

Mountjoy Square was once one of Dublin's most handsome squares, lined with terraced, red-brick Georgian houses that still have a dishevelled elegance. From its northwestern corner, walk down Gardiner Pl and right on North Temple St to see the fine, now deconsecrated, Georgian **St George's Church**, designed by architect Francis Johnston.

❷ Garden of Remembrance

Take a left onto Hardwicke St and left again onto North Frederick St, past the **Abbey Presbyterian Church**. Take a peek inside the Garden of Remembrance, opened in 1966 to commemorate the 50th anniversary of the 1916 Easter Rising.

❸ Dublin City Gallery – the Hugh Lane

Facing the gardens is Dublin's premier modern art gallery, the **Dublin City Gallery – the Hugh Lane** (p98).

The southern part of the square is occupied by the **Rotunda Hospital**, a wonderful example of public architecture in the Georgian style.

④ General Post Office

Head south down O'Connell St, passing the 120m-high **Spire**. On the western side of O'Connell St is the stunning neoclassical **General Post Office** (p102), which made history as the HQ of the Easter Rising – you can still see bullet holes in the columns.

⑤ Four Courts

When you hit the river, turn right and walk west, past the **Ha'penny Bridge** (named for the charge levied on those who used it), to reach the **Four Courts** (p102), one of James Gandon's Georgian masterpieces and home to the highest court in the country.

⑥ St Michan's Church

Finally take a right onto Church St to visit **St Michan's Church**, a beautiful Georgian construction with grisly vaults populated by the remains of the long departed.

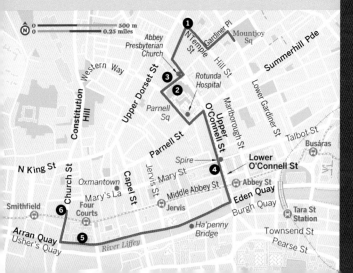

Best Walks
Viking & Medieval Dublin

🏃 The Walk

If you build a city out of wood and mud, there's little chance it'll survive through the ages. So it was with the original Viking settlement of Dublin, but if you look closely there are still vestiges of the city's Norse past. The medieval city fared much better, mostly because stone was the primarily building block.

Start Essex Gate, Parliament St

Finish Dublin Castle

Length 2.5km; two hours

🍴 Take a Break

Banyi Japanese Dining (p74), down a cobbled alley in Temple Bar, is the best Japanese restaurant in town – the lunch bento alone is an absolute treat.

St Audoen's Church

❶ **Essex Gate**

Once a main entrance gate to the city, the only sign of **Essex Gate** is a bronze plaque where it stood. Further along, you can see the original foundations of **Isolde's Tower** through a grill in the pavement, in front of the Czech Inn pub.

❷ **Brazen Head**

Head north down to the river and proceed west along Merchant's Quay. Opposite **Father Mathew Bridge** (built in 1818 on the spot that gave the city its Irish name, Baile Átha Cliath, or Town of the Hurdle Ford) is Dublin's oldest pub, the **Brazen Head** (p93), established in 1198, though the present building is positively youthful dating from 1668.

❸ **St Audoen's Church**

Take the next left onto Cook St to examine St Audoen's Arch (1240), the only remaining medieval gate of the 32 that were built. Climb up the ramparts to the city's oldest existing church, St Audoen's.

It was built around 1190, and is not to be confused with the newer Catholic church next door.

❹ Dublinia

Leave the little park, join High St and head east until you reach the first corner. Here on your left is the former Synod Hall, now **Dublinia: Experience Viking & Medieval Dublin** (p72), where the original settlement has been interactively re-created.

❺ The Two Cathedrals

Next to Dublinia, **Christ Church Cathedral** (p66) was the most important medieval church *inside* the medieval walls; about 300m south along Nicholas St (which becomes Patrick St) stands the most important church *outside* the city walls, **St Patrick's Cathedral** (p82).

❻ Dublin Castle

Finally, follow our route up Bride, Werburgh and Castle Sts, and finish up with a long wander around **Dublin Castle** (p28), the fortification that defined and protected medieval Dublin.

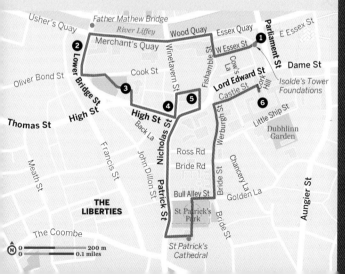

Best
Eating

The choice of restaurants in Dublin has never been better. Every cuisine and every trend – from doughnuts on the run to kale with absolutely everything – is catered for, as the city seeks to satisfy the discerning taste buds of its diners.

A Typical Meal?

Most meals are meat-based, with beef, lamb and pork common options. The most Dublin of dishes is coddle, a working-class concoction of bacon rashers, sausages, onions, potato and plenty of black pepper. More easily available is the national edible icon, Irish stew, the slow-simmered one-pot wonder of lamb, potatoes, onions, parsley and thyme (note, no carrots).

Irish Bread

The most famous Irish bread, and one of the signature tastes of Ireland, is soda bread. Irish flour is soft and doesn't take well to yeast as a raising agent, so Irish bakers of the 19th century leavened their bread with bicarbonate of soda. Combined with buttermilk, it makes a superbly light-textured and tasty bread, and is often on the breakfast menus at B&Bs. Scones, tarts and biscuits are specialities too.

☑ **Top Tips**

Restaurants usually open noon to 11pm (or midnight); food service generally ends around 10pm. Top-end restaurants often close between 3pm and 6pm; restaurants serving brunch open around 10am.

Best Modern Irish

Chapter One Nobody knew Irish cuisine could taste this good! (p106)

Winding Stair Classic Irish dishes given an elegant twist. (p109)

Union8 Beautifully presented modern Irish cuisine. (p91)

Workshop Gastropub The standard bearer

Traditional soda bread

for pub grub in Dublin. (p117)

L Mulligan Grocer A pub that does terrific new Irish cuisine. (p106)

Best Formal Dining

Chapter One The food is sublime, the atmosphere is wonderfully relaxed. (p106)

L'Ecrivain Excellent cuisine à la française. (p61)

Restaurant Patrick Guilbaud Perhaps the best restaurant in Ireland, where everything is just right. (p60)

Greenhouse Michelin-starred and marvellous:

Irish meets Scandinavian. (p41)

Best Casual Bites

Fumbally Great warehouse space with filling sandwiches and good coffee. (p89)

M&L The most authentic Chinese restaurant in town. (p104)

Paulie's Pizza Gourmet pizzas like you'd get in Italy...or New York City. (p117)

Oxmantown Great sandwiches and breakfasts, with locally baked bread. (p104)

Pepper Pot Balcony cafe that does sensational

organic eggs as well as other dishes. (p41)

Best Midrange Restaurants

Coburg Brasserie French-influenced, mostly seafood brasserie. (p59)

Pichet Modern French cuisine done to perfection. (p41)

Banyi Japanese Dining The best Japanese food in town. (p74)

Fish Shop Exquisitely fresh seafood at this tiny restaurant. (p105)

Juniors Deli & Cafe New York–style Italian restaurant. (p117)

Best Drinking & Nightlife

If there's one constant about life in Dublin, it's that Dubliners will always take a drink. Come hell or high water, the city's pubs will never be short of customers, and we suspect that exploring a variety of Dublin's legendary pubs and bars ranks pretty high on the list of reasons you're here.

Pub or Bar?

There are pubs for every taste and sensibility, although the traditional haunts populated by flat-capped pensioners bursting with insightful anecdotes are about as rare as hen's teeth and most Dubliners select their favourite from a wide selection of trendy bars, designer boozers and hipster locales. But despair not, for it is not the spit or sawdust that makes a great Dublin pub but the patrons themselves, who provide a reassuring guarantee that Dublin's reputation as the pub capital of the world remains in perfectly safe (if occasionally unsteady!) hands.

Pub Etiquette

The rounds system – the simple custom where someone buys you a drink and you buy one back – is the bedrock of Irish pub culture. It's summed up in the Irish saying: 'It's impossible for two men to go to a pub for one drink.' Nothing will hasten your fall from social grace here like the failure to uphold this pub law. The Irish are extremely generous and one thing they can't abide is tight-fistedness.

Another golden rule about the system is that the next round starts when the first person has finished (or preferably just about to finish) their drink. It doesn't matter if you're only halfway through your pint, if it's your round, get them in.

Best Traditional Pubs

John Mulligan's The gold standard of traditional. (p117)

Long Hall Stylishly old-fashioned. (p42)

Stag's Head Popular with journalists and students. (p44)

Old Royal Oak A proper neighbourhood pub. (p91)

Walshe's The only concession to modernity is the young clientele's clothing! (p107)

John Mulligan's pub

Best Pint of Guinness

Kehoe's Stalwart popular with locals and tourists. (p42)

John Mulligan's Perfect setting for a perfect pint. (p117)

Grogan's Castle Lounge Great because the locals demand it! (p42)

Fallon's Centuries of experience. (p91)

Best Live Music

O'Donoghue's The unofficial HQ of folk music. (p63)

Cobblestone Best sessions in town. (p106)

Auld Dubliner Trad sessions for tourists. (p75)

Best Contemporary Bars

Vintage Cocktail Club Spruced up speakeasy. (p75)

Liquor Rooms Cavernous basement haunt. (p74)

Chelsea Drug Store Art-deco hang-out. (p42)

P.Mac's Old-style new hipster hang-out. (p43)

Farrier & Draper Georgian elegance meets Prohibition-era style. (p43)

Worth a Trip

A contender for best pub in Dublin is **John Kavanagh's** (Gravediggers; 01-830 7978; 1 Prospect Sq; 13, 19, 19A from O'Connell St) of Glasnevin, more commonly known as the Gravediggers because the employees from the adjacent cemetery had a secret serving hatch so that they could drink on the job. An absolute classic.

Best
Museums &
Galleries

It's hardly surprising that Ireland's capital and biggest city by far should have the bulk of the best museums and galleries, but even so Dublin operates a cultural surplus. You can uncover the city's – and nation's – history, examine its most important artefacts and gaze upon art from prehistory to the modern day.

Admission & Access

All of the city's main museums and galleries are free to explore, including the National Gallery, the Dublin City Art Gallery – the Hugh Lane, the Irish Museum of Modern Art and the various august bodies collected under the umbrella of the National Museum of Ireland. Heritage sites such as Kilmainham Gaol and the two cathedrals charge admission. Opening hours are generally from 9.30am or 10am to 5pm or 5.30pm from Monday to Saturday, with later opening (usually until 7pm) on Thursday, and afternoon openings only on Sunday.

Dublin Pass

For heavy-duty sightseeing, the **Dublin Pass** (www.dublinpass.com; adult/child day €52/31, 3 day €83/52) will save you a packet. It provides free entry to more than 25 attractions (including the Guinness Storehouse), discounts at 20 others and guaranteed fast-track entry to some of the busiest sights. To avail of the free Aircoach transfer to and from the airport, order the card online so you have it when you land. Otherwise, it's available from any Discover Ireland Dublin Tourism Centre.

Best Collections

Dublin City Gallery – Hugh Lane Impressive collection of modern and contemporary Irish art. (p98)

National Gallery The best collection of classical European and Irish art in the country. (p54)

National Museum of Ireland – Archaeology Ór – Ireland's Gold is the finest collection of Celtic art in the world. (p52)

Irish Museum of Modern Art Important collection of contemporary Irish art. (p88)

National Museum of Ireland – Decorative Arts & History The social and military history of Ireland told through clothing, jewellery and uniforms. (p102)

National Gallery

Best Small Museums

Marsh's Library An 18th-century library that hasn't changed a bit since it opened. (p88)

Chester Beatty Library Fabulous collection of books, scrolls and antique objets d'art from all over the world. (p32)

Little Museum of Dublin Fascinating items crowd-sourced from Dubliners make this a most compelling visit. (p38)

Teeling Distillery A distillery with a hands-on look at how whiskey is made. (p88, pictured above left)

Best Interactive Experience

Guinness Storehouse You get to actually drink a Guinness at the source. (p80)

Old Jameson Distillery The whiskey-tasting experience at the end of the tour is great fun – if you're over 18. (p102)

Irish Family History Centre Explore your Irish roots through interactive screens. (p116)

Best
Entertainment

Need a good night out? Dublin's got you covered, whether you want an evening with a string quartet or to sweat it out on the dance floor at 3am.There's something on every night, especially relating to music, which is undoubtedly one of Dublin's strongest suits.

Best For Rock & Pop

Workman's Club A great spot for left-of-centre live music, from electronica to alt rock and beardy folk. (p76)

Whelan's The spiritual home of the singer-songwriter; you can get up close and personal at this terrifically intimate venue. (p44)

Vicar Street A midsize venue that generally hosts soul, folk and world music. (p93; pictured, Bell XI performing at Vicar Street)

3 Arena The place to see your favourite touring international superstar, along with 23,000 others. (p119)

Best for Theatre

Gate Theatre Box office international and Irish plays, with the occasional visiting star. (p109)

Abbey Theatre An emphasis on Irish works, both old and new. (p109)

Project Arts Centre Mostly experimental and new theatre. (p76)

Best Online Listings

Entertainment.ie (www.entertainment.ie) For all events.

MCD (www.mcd.ie) Biggest promoter in Ireland.

Sweebe (www.sweebe.com) More than 200 venues listed.

Totally Dublin (www.totallydublin.ie) Comprehensive listings and reviews.

☑ Top Tips

▶ Theatre, comedy and classical concerts are usually booked directly through the venue.

▶ Tickets to big gigs are sold at the venue or through **Ticket-Master** (☎0818 719 300; www.ticketmaster.ie; Stephen's Green Shopping Centre; 🚉all city centre, 🚆St Stephen's Green). Note it charges between 9% and 12.5% service charge per ticket.

What's On In (www.whatsonin.ie) From markets to gigs and club nights.

Best
Markets

In recent years Dublin has gone gaga for markets. Which is kind of ironic, considering the city's traditional markets, such as Moore St, were ignored by those same folks who now can't get enough of the homemade hummus on sale at the new gourmet spots. It's all so...continental.

CAROLIN VOELKER/GETTY IMAGES ©

Self-Catering

Dublin's choice of artisan street and covered markets continues to improve. There are some excellent options, especially south of the river, including a fine selection of cheesemongers and bakeries. North of the river, the traditional Moore Street Market is the city's most famous, where the colour of the produce is matched by the language of the hawkers.

Best Markets

Temple Bar Book Market Rummage through secondhand books. (p77)

Temple Bar Food Market The city's best open-air food market. (p76)

Moore Street Market Open-air, steadfastly 'Old Dublin' market, with fruit, fish and flowers. (p109)

☑ **Top Tip**

▶ Dubliners don't haggle...much. Generally speaking, the price you see is the price you'll pay, but occasionally there'll be a little wiggle room, especially if you're buying more than one item: 'Tell you what, love', the trader might say, 'I'll give you the pair of them for €20 (on items priced at €21). Can't say fairer than that!'

Best
Gay & Lesbian

Dublin is a pretty good place to be LGBTQ. Being gay or lesbian in the city is completely unremarkable, while in recent years members of the trans community have also found greater acceptance. The passage of the Marriage Equality Act in 2015 was a major hallmark for gay rights.

Best Nightlife

George The biggest, brashest and most popular of the city's gay bars. (p44)

Pantibar Alternative drag shows, make-and-do nights and a basement pool room make this a popular spot. (p107)

Best Resources

Gaire Online message board and resource centre (www.gaire.com).

Gay Men's Health Project Practical advice on men's health issues. (www.hse.ie/go/GMHS).

Gay Switchboard Dublin A friendly and useful voluntary service that provides information on matters such as legal issues and where to find accommodation. (www.gayswitchboard.ie)

National Lesbian & Gay Federation Publishers of *Gay Community News*. (www.nxf.ie)

☑ **Top Tip**

▶ If you do encounter any sort of trouble, call the **Garda LGBTQ Liaison Officer** (☎116006; ⊙24hr) or the **Sexual Assault Unit** (☎01-666 3430; ⊙24hr).

Outhouse Top gay, lesbian and bisexual resource centre. (www.outhouse.ie)

Best
Festivals

Dublin enjoys a good celebration – of food, theatre, music and, of course, St Patrick, which is the mother of all festivals and takes place over four days instead of the traditional one.

AITORMMG/PHOTO/SHUTTERSTOCK ©

Best Festivals

Dublin Fringe Festival Best (and worst) of contemporary theatre. (www.fringefest.com; ☺ Sep)

St Patrick's Festival Dublin goes a bit wild for four days. (www.stpatricksfestival.ie; ☺ Mar)

Culture Night One night extravaganza of culture, talks and performances. (www.culturenight.ie; ☺ Sep)

Forbidden Fruit Alternative music festival. (www.forbiddenfruit.ie; ☺ Jun)

Longitude Dublin's version of Glastonbury. (www.longitude.ie; ☺ Jul)

Dublin Pride Two weeks of LGBTQ fun. (www.dublinpride.ie; ☺ mid-Jun)

Taste of Dublin Excellent food fair. (www.tasteofdublin.ie; ☺ mid-Jun)

Only in Dublin

All-Ireland Finals Climax of hurling and Gaelic football championships, on first and third Sunday of September, respectively.

Bloomsday Leopold Bloom's saunter through Dublin is celebrated. (www.jamesjoyce.ie)

Liffey Swim Five hundred lunatics swim 2.5km from Rory O'More Bridge to the Custom House in late August – one can't but admire their steel will (www.leinsteropensea.ie).

☑ **Top Tip**

▶ Book tickets in advance for the bigger music festivals such as Forbidden Fruit and Longitude; and for the fringe festival – good luck landing All-Ireland tickets!

Christmas Dip at the Forty Foot At 11am on Christmas Day, a group of very brave swimmers jump into the icy waters at the Forty Foot, just below the Martello Tower in the southern suburb of Sandycove, for a 20-minute swim to the rocks and back.

Best
Parks & Gardens

Dublin's collection of green spaces includes a handful of beautifully manicured Georgian squares, some lovely grassy patches along the river and even a couple of nice museum gardens. But they all pale in comparison to the Phoenix Park, Europe's largest enclosed city park, which dominates the northwestern edge of the city and is a favourite weekend playground. All but one (Fitzwilliam Sq) are open to the public.

St Stephen's Green The city's favourite sun trap, with every blade of its manicured lawns occupied by lounge lizards and lunchers. (p38)

Merrion Square Perfectly raked paths meander by beautifully maintained lawns and flower beds. (p57)

Phoenix Park Dublin's biggest park, home to deer, the zoo, the president and the US ambassador. (p95)

Iveagh Gardens Delightful, slightly dishevelled gardens hidden behind St Stephen's Green. (p35, pictured above left)

War Memorial Gardens The best-kept open secret in town are these magnificent gardens by the Liffey. (p89)

Herbert Park This extensive park is one of the most popular green lungs south of the Liffey. (p123)

☑ **Top Tips**

▶ All the public squares are open only during daylight hours.

▶ Phoenix Park is open 24 hours, but it's not recommended after dusk unless you're in a vehicle.

Best
For Kids

Kid-friendly? You bet. Dublin loves the little 'uns, and will enthusiastically 'ooh' and 'aah' at the cuteness of your progeny. But alas such admiration hasn't fully translated into child services such as widespread and accessible baby-changing facilities.

LARRYDJ/SHUTTERSTOCK ©

Attractions & Admissions

Most attractions have a children's admission fee usually for under-16s; those aged between 16 and 18 can often benefit from a student price. Most attractions also offer a family ticket, which usually means two adults and two children under 16.

Resources

Parents with young children should check out www.eumom. com; an excellent site about family-friendly accommodation is www. babygoes2.com.

Best Attractions for Kids

Dublinia Interactive exhibits that are specifically designed to appeal to younger visitors. (p72)

Ark Children's Cultural Centre Fun, educational activities for kids aged three to 14. (p72)

Dublin Zoo Visit 400 animals from 100 different species in one of Europe's better zoos. (p95, pictured above)

☑ **Top Tips**

▶ Children under five travel free on all public transport.

▶ Unaccompanied minors are not allowed in pubs; accompanied children can remain until 9pm (10pm May to September).

Best
Architecture

Dublin's skyline is a clue to its age, with visible peaks of its architectural history dating back to the Middle Ages. Dublin is older still, but there are few traces left of its Viking origins and you'll have to begin your architectural exploration in the 12th century. Dublin's architectural apotheosis came in the 18th century, during the Georgian era.

Best Georgian

Leinster House Richard Cassels built this home for the Duke of Leinster; now home to the Irish parliament. (p58, pictured above left)

Charlemont House Lord Charlemont's city dwelling, now home to the Dublin City Gallery – the Hugh Lane, was one of the city's finest Georgian homes. (p98)

Powerscourt Townhouse Shopping Centre Once home to third Viscount Powerscourt, Robert Mack's beautiful building is now a popular shopping centre. (p48)

Four Courts The home of the highest courts in the land is the joint effort of Thomas Cooley and James Gandon. (p102)

Custom House James Gandon announced his arrival in Dublin with this architectural stunner. (p115)

Bank of Ireland Now a bank, it was designed by Edward Lovett Pearce for the Irish parliament. (p39)

Best Modern

Bord Gáis Energy Theatre (2010) Daniel Libeskind brought some serious architectural

chops to his elegant design for this 2100-capacity theatre. (p119)

Convention Centre (2011) Kevin Roche's eye-catching design features a huge glass 'tube' set at a 45-degree angle in the building. (p113)

Samuel Beckett Bridge (2007) Spanish architect Santiago Calatrava's wishbone design structure in the Docklands at Spencer Dock. (p113)

Grand Canal Square (2007) Martha Schwartz' beautifully designed square fronting the Bord Gáis is the city's most beautiful modern space. (p113)

Best **For Free**

Dublin has a reputation for being expensive and there's no doubt you can haemorrhage cash without too much effort. But the good news is you can see and experience much of what's great about Dublin without having to spend a cent.

DESIGN PICS/GEORGE MUNDAY ©

Culture Night

For one night a year, museums, galleries, artists' studios, historic homes and churches come together for **Culture Night** (www.culturenight.ie; Sep) and open their doors and host performances, lectures and workshops for the public. Everything is free and fabulous.

Best Free Museums

National Museum of Ireland All three Dublin branches of the National Museum – **Archaeology**, **Decorative Arts & History** and **Natural History** – are free of charge. (p52) (p102) (p57)

National Gallery The State's proud collection

of art is well-represented on the walls of the National Gallery. (p54)

Dublin City Gallery – Hugh Lane This extraordinary collection of modern art is free to peruse. (p98)

Irish Museum of Modern Art Ireland's foremost collection of

contemporary art is available to all at no cost. (p88, pictured above right)

Chester Beatty Library A treasure trove of ancient books, illuminated manuscripts, precious scrolls and other gorgeous objets d'art. (p32)

Science Gallery Tap into your inner nerd and discover how interesting it all is...for absolutely nothing. (p27)

Best **Tours**

Best Walking Tours

Historical Walking Tour
Excellent two-hour tours led by Trinity graduates. (☎ 01-878 0227; www. historicaltours.ie; Trinity College Gate; adult/student/ child €12/10/free; ⏱ 11am & 3pm May-Sep, 11am Apr & Oct, 11am Fri-Sun Nov-Mar; 🚊 all city centre)

Dublin Literary Pub Crawl
An evening tour of pubs associated with famous Dublin writers is a sure-fire recipe for success. (☎ 01-670 5602; www.dublinpubcrawl.com; 9 Duke St; adult/student €13/11; ⏱ 7.30pm daily Apr-Oct, 7.30pm Thu-Sun Nov-Mar; 🚊 all city centre)

Dublin Musical Pub Crawl
Explore the history of Irish traditional music with two expert musicians. (☎ 01-478 0193; www.discoverdublin.ie; 58-59 Fleet St; adult/student €14/12; ⏱ 7.30pm daily Apr-Oct, 7.30pm Thu-Sat Nov-Mar; 🚊 all city centre)

Pat Liddy Walking Tours
Variety of themed tours led by Dublin's best-known tour guide. (☎ 01-831 1109; www. walkingtours.ie; Visit Dublin Centre, 25 Suffolk St; tours €10-15; 🚊 all city centre)

Green Mile
Excellent one-hour tour of St Stephen's Green led by local historian Donal Fallon. (☎ 01-661 1000; www.littlemuseum.ie; Little Museum of Dublin, 15 St Stephen's Green N; adult/student €7/5; ⏱ 11am Sat & Sun; 🚊 all city centre, 🚋 St Stephen's Green)

Fab Food Trails
Excellent tasting walks exploring independent producers. (www.fabfoodtrails.ie; tours €55; ⏱ 10am Sat)

Best Bike Tour

See Dublin by Bike
Three-hour themed tours that take in the city's highlights and not-so-obvious sights. (☎ 01-280 1899; www.seedublinbybike. ie; Daintree Bldg, Pleasants Pl; tours €25; 🚊 all city centre)

Best Bus Tours

City Sightseeing
One-and-a-half-hour tour that includes the city centre, the Guinness Storehouse and the north quays

☑ Top Tip

▶ Dublin Visitor Centre has put together an app (for iPhone and Android) with four themed walking tours covering Dublin's history over the last 200 years.

via the entrance to the Phoenix Park. (www. citysightseeingdublin.ie; 14 Upper O'Connell St; adult/student €19/17; 🚊 all city centre, 🚋 Abbey)

Dublin Bus Tours
Offers a variety of tours, including the hop-on, hop-off Dublin City Tour, Ghost Bus Tour, and Coast and Castles Tour. (☎ 01-872 0000; www. dublinsightseeing.ie; 59 Upper O'Connell St; adult €15-28; 🚊 all city centre, 🚋 Abbey)

Survival Guide

Survival Guide

Before You Go

When to Go

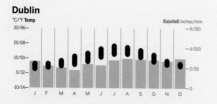

Dublin

°C/°F Temp   Rainfall inches/mm

➡ **High season (Jun–mid-Sep)** Weather at its best; accommodation rates at their highest (especially August).

➡ **Shoulder (Easter–end May, mid-Sep–end Oct)** Weather often good, sun and rain in May. 'Indian summers' and often warm in September; summer crowds and accommodation rates drop off .

➡ **Low season (Nov–Feb)** Fewer crowds; weather at its coldest and wettest; attractions operate as normal.

Book Your Stay

Useful Websites

➡ **All Dublin Hotels** (www.irelandhotels.com/hotels) Decent spread of accommodation in the ci centre and suburbs.

➡ **Dublin Tourism** (www.visitdublin.com) Good selection of rated accommodation.

➡ **Lonely Planet** (www.lonelyplanet.com/irelanc dublin/hotels) Recommendations and booking

Best Budget

Trinity Lodge (www.trinitylodge.com) Comfy and central B&B.

Isaacs Hostel (www.isaacs.ie) Best bunks in the city.

Generator Hostel (www.generatorhostels.com) Funky hostel on the north side.

Ariel House (www.ariel-house.net) Luxury B&B ir Ballsbridge.

est Midrange

adisson Blu Royal
otel (www.radisson
u.ie/royalhotel-dublin)
wanky spot for busi-
ss.

liff Townhouse (www.
eclifftownhouse.com)
errific boutique bolt-
ole.

berdeen Lodge (www.
berdeenlodgedublin.
m) Hospitality at its
est.

ean (www.deanhotel
ublin.ie) Trendy designer
otel.

est Top End

lerrion (www.merrion-
otel.com) Sophisticated,
egant and central.

tzwilliam Hotel (www.
tzwilliam-hotel.com)
odern and very tasteful.

onrad Dublin (www.
nradhotels.com) Su-
erb, modern rooms.

ish Landmark Trust
www.irishlandmark.
m) Two stunning
8th-century heritage
omes.

umber 31 (www.num-
er31.ie) Exquisite hotel
at combines Georgian
egance with 60s style.

Arriving in Dublin

Dublin Airport

➡ Located 13km north of
the city centre, **Dublin**
Airport (📞 01-814 1111;
www.dublinairport.com) has
direct connections to
most major European
cities and about a dozen
cities in North America.

➡ **Aircoach** (📞 01-844
7118; www.aircoach.ie; One
way/return €7/12) Private
coach service with three
routes from the airport
to over 20 destinations
throughout the city.
Coaches run every 10 to
15 minutes between 6am
and midnight, then hourly
from midnight until 6am.

➡ **Airlink Express Coach**
(📞 01-873 4222; www.dublin
bus.ie; One way/return €6/10)
Bus 747 runs every 10 to
20 minutes from 5.45am
to 12.30am between
airport, the central bus
station (Busáras) and
the Dublin Bus office on
Upper O'Connell St. Bus
757 runs every 15 to 30
minutes from 5am to
12.25am between airport
and various stops in the
city.

➡ **Taxi** To city centre
should take about 45

minutes and cost around
€25, including an initial
charge of €3.60 (€4
between 10pm and 8am
and on Sundays and bank
holidays).

Dublin Port

➡ The **Dublin Port**
Terminal (📞 01-855 2222;
Alexandra Rd; 🚌 53 from
Talbot St) is 3km northeast
of the city centre.

➡ An express bus transfer
to and from Dublin Port
is operated by **Morton's**
(www.mortonscoaches.
ie; adult/child €3/1.50;
🕐 7.15am, 1.30pm & 7pm),
departing from West-
moreland St at 7.15am,
1.30pm and 7pm (timed
to coincide with ferry
departures).

Getting Around

Bus

➡ Buses run from
around 6am (some start
at 5.30am) to about
11.30pm. The **Dublin Bus**
Office (Map p100; 📞 01-873
4222; www.dublinbus.
ie; 59 Upper O'Connell St;
🕐 8.30am-5.30pm Tue-Fri, to
2pm Sat, 9am-5.30pm Mon;
🚌 all city centre) has a free
app for all of its services.

➡ Fares are calculated according to stages (stops), from €2 (1-3 stages) to €3.30 (more than 13 stages).

➡ Buses only take exact change or a **Leap Card** (www.leapcard.ie), available from most newsagents, which is 20% cheaper than cash fare.

➡ Nitelink late-night services (€6.50; €5.20 with Leap Card) run every 20 minutes from 12.30am to 4.30am Friday and Saturday from the city centre; see www.dublinbus.ie for route details.

Tram

➡ The **Luas** (www.luas.ie) light-rail system has two lines: the green line (running every five to 15 minutes) connects St Stephen's Green with Sandyford in south Dublin via Ranelagh and Dundrum; the red line (every 20 minutes) runs from the Point Village to Tallaght via the north quays and Heuston Station. In 2017 they were linked by a new cross-city line through the city centre.

➡ Ticket machines at every stop; a typical short-hop fare (around four stops) is €2.30.

➡ Services run from 5.30am to 12.30am Monday to Friday, from 6.30am to 12.30am Saturday and from 7am to 11.30pm Sunday.

Train

➡ **Dublin Area Rapid Transport** (DART; ☎01-836 6222; www.irishrail.ie) provides quick train access to the coast as far north as Howth (about 30 minutes) and as far south as Greystones in County Wicklow.

➡ Every 10 to 20 minutes, sometimes even more frequently, from around 6.30am to midnight Monday to Saturday. Services are less frequent on Sunday.

➡ A one-way DART ticket from Dublin to Dun Laoghaire or Howth costs €3.25.

Bike

➡ **Dublinbikes** (www.dublinbikes.ie), a public bicycle-rental scheme with more than 100 stations spread across the city centre.

➡ Purchase a €10 smart card (as well as pay a credit-card deposit of €150) or a three-day card online or at any station

before 'freeing' a bike for use, which is then free of charge for the first 30 minutes and €0.50 for each half-hour thereafter.

➡ Bicycle lanes are marked rust-red but are intermittent and are encroached upon by motorised traffic.

➡ Basic traffic infractions by cyclists are subject to a spot €40 fine.

➡ Helmets and high-visibility clothing not compulsory; lights after dusk are.

Car & Motorcycle

➡ Traffic in Dublin is a nightmare and parking is an expensive headache.

➡ No free spots to park anywhere in the city centre during business hours (7am to 7pm Monday to Saturday); paid parking priced according to zone: €2.90 per hour in yellow (central) zone down to €0.60 in blue (suburban).

➡ Supervised and sheltered car parks cost around €4 per hour, with most offering a low-cost evening flat rate.

➡ Clamping of illegally parked cars is thoroughly enforced, and there is an €80 charge for removal.

Free parking after 7pm
Monday to Saturday, and
all day Sunday, in most
metered spots (unless
indicated) and on single
yellow lines.

All the main car rental
agencies are represented
in Dublin, including **Hertz**
(☑ 01-844 5466; www.hertz.
com; Dublin Airport; ☺5am-
midnight). **Avis** (☑01-605 7500;
www.avis.ie; 35 Old Kilmainham Rd; ☺8.30am-5.45pm
Mon-Fri, 8.30am-2.30pm
Sat & Sun; ☒23, 25, 25A,
66, 68, 69 from city centre),
Budget (☑01-837 9611;
www.budget.ie; 151 Lower
Drumcondra Rd; ☺9am-6pm;
☒41 from O'Connell St),
Europcar (☑01-812 2880;
www.europcar.ie; Dublin
Airport; ☺5am-1am) and
Thrifty (☑01-840 0800;
www.thrifty.ie; Dublin Airport;
☺5am-1am).

Essential Information

Business Hours

Banks 10am to 4pm
Monday to Friday (to 5pm
Thursday).

Offices 9am to 5pm
Monday to Friday.

Post offices 9am to 6pm
Monday to Friday, 9am to
1pm Saturday.

Restaurants Noon to
10pm (or midnight); food
service generally ends
around 9pm.

Shops 9.30am to 6pm
Monday to Saturday (to
8pm Thursday, to 9pm
for the bigger shopping
centres and super-
markets), noon to 6pm
Sunday.

Discount Cards

Dublin Pass (adult/child
per day €52/31, 3 days
€83/52) Free entry to
more than 25 attractions
(including the Guinness
Storehouse), discounts
at 20 others and guar-
anteed fast-track entry
to some of the busiest
sights. To avail of the free
Aircoach transfer to and
from the airport, order
the card online so you
have it when you land.
Otherwise, it's available
from any Discover Ireland
Dublin Tourism Centre.

Heritage Card (adult/
child & student €40/10)
This card entitles you to
free access to all sights
in and around Dublin
managed by the Office

of Public Works (OPW).
You can buy it at OPW
sites or Dublin Tourism
offices.

Electricity

**Type G
230V/50Hz**

Money

Currency
➡ Euro (€)

ATMs
➡ ATMs are widespread
throughout the city,
including in many
convenience stores and
some pubs.

Credit Cards

→ Visa and MasterCard credit and debit cards are widely accepted.

→ Smaller businesses prefer debit cards (and will charge a fee for credit cards).

→ Nearly all credit and debit cards use the chip-and-PIN system and an increasing number of places will not accept cards that don't.

Changing Money

→ Best exchange rates are at banks, although bureaux de change and other exchange facilities usually open for more hours.

Money-Saving Tips

→ Many restaurants do good-value lunch deals and early-bird specials.

→ Buy a **Leap Card** (www.leapcard.ie) if you're going to use the bus; it's cheaper than a cash fare.

→ Buy your tickets for fee-charging attractions online to avail of discounts.

→ There's a cluster of banks located around College Green opposite Trinity College and all have exchange facilities.

Tipping

Hotels Only for bellhops who carry luggage, then €1 per bag.

Pubs Not expected unless table service is provided, then €1 for a round of drinks.

Restaurants Tip 10% for decent service, up to 15% in more expensive places.

Taxis Tip 10% or round up to the nearest euro.

Toilet attendants Tip €0.50.

Public Holidays

New Year's Day
1 January

St Patrick's Day
17 March

Easter (Good Friday to Easter Monday inclusive) March/April

May Bank Holiday 1 May

June Bank Holiday First Monday in June

August Bank Holiday First Monday in August

October Bank Holiday Last Monday in October

Christmas Day
25 December

St Stephen's Day
26 December

Safe Travel

→ Don't leave anything visible in your car when you park.

→ Skimming at ATMs is a ongoing problem; be sure to cover the keypad with your hand when you inpu your PIN.

→ The western edge of Thomas St (onto James St) can be a bit dodgy due to the presence of drug addicts.

→ The northern end of Gardiner St, along with the areas northeast of there, have crime-related problems.

Toilets

→ There are no on-street facilities in Dublin.

→ All shopping centres have public toilets; if you're stranded, go into any bar or hotel.

Tourist Informatio

→ **Dublin Visitor Centre** (Map p36; www. visitdublin.com; 25 Suffolk St; ⏱9am-5.30pm Mon-Sat 10.30am-3pm Sun; 🚌all

y centre) General visitor
formation on Dublin
nd Ireland, as well as
ccommodation and
ooking service.

A handful of official-
oking tourism offices
n Grafton and O'Connell
ts are actually privately
n enterprises where
embers pay to be
cluded.

ravellers with isabilities

Most DART stations
e disabled-friendly,
ART and train services
quire 24 hours' notice
efore boarding with a
heelchair.

All city buses are wheel-
hair-accessible, but
uas is the way to go for
aximum accessibility.

Ireland.com (www.
eland.com/en-us/
ccommodation/articles/
ccessibility) Informa-
ve article with links to
ccessibility information
r transport and tourist
tractions.

Mobility Mojo (www.
obilitymojo.com)
ore than 500 reviews

of establishments in a
searchable database.

➡ **Trip-Ability** (www.
trip-ability.com) Review
site which should soon
feature a booking facility.

➡ **Accessible Ireland**
(www.accessibleireland.
com) Reviews, plus short
introductions to public
transport.

➡ **Irish Wheelchair
Association** (☎01-818
6400; www.iwa.ie; Áras
Chúchulain, Blackheath Dr,
Clontarf; ☺9am-5.30pm
Mon-Fri) Useful national
association.

➡ Download Lonely
Planet's free Accessible

Travel guides from http://
lptravel.to/Accessible-
Travel.

Visas

➡ Not required for
citizens of Australia,
New Zealand, the USA
or Canada, or citizens of
European nations that
belong to the European
Economic Area (EEA).

➡ Citizens of Australia,
Canada, New Zealand,
South Africa and the US
can visit Ireland for up to
three months without a
visa. They are not allowed
to work unless sponsored
by an employer.

Dos & Don'ts

Greetings Shake hands with both men and
women when meeting for the first time. Female
friends are greeted with a single kiss on the
cheek.

Queues Dubliners can be a little lax about
proper queuing etiquette, but are not shy about
confronting queue-skippers who jump in front
of them.

Polite requests Dubliners often use 'Sorry' instead of 'Excuse me' when asking for something;
they're not really apologising for anything.

Behind the Scenes

Send Us Your Feedback

We love to hear from travellers – your comments help make our books better. We read every word, and we guarantee that your feedback goes straight to the authors. Visit **lonelyplanet.com/contact** to submit your updates and suggestions.

Note: We may edit, reproduce and incorporate your comments in Lonely Planet products such as guidebooks, websites and digital products, so let us know if you don't want your comments reproduced or your name acknowledged. For a copy of our privacy policy visit lonelyplanet.com/privacy.

Fionn Davenport's Thanks

Thanks to everyone in Dublin who helped with research, to Laura for constantly picking me up from the airport and to LP editors for indulging my every misstep.

Acknowledgements

Cover photograph: Old Library, Trinity College; E+/Getty ©
Contents photograph (pp4–5): Inner yard, Dublin Castle; Kraft_Stoff/Shutterstock ©

This Book

This 4th edition of Lonely Planet's *Pocket Dublin* guidebook was researched and written by Fionn Davenport. The previous edition was written by Fionn with additional research by Neil Wilson. This guidebook was produced by the following:

Destination Editor James Smart

Product Editors Ronan Abayawickrema, Sandie Kestell

Regional Senior Cartographer Mark Griffiths

Book Designer Gwen Cotter

Assisting Editors Imogen Bannister, Michelle Bennett, Nigel Chin, Melanie Dankel, Andrea Dobbin, Helen Koehne, Chris Pitts

Cover Researcher Campbell McKenzie

Thanks to Stephen Cluskey, Noelle Daly, Martin Heng, AnneMarie McCarthy, Genna Patterson, Jessica Ryan, Angela Tinson, Tony Wheeler

ndex

See also separate subindexes for:

⊗ Eating p158

🍸 Drinking p158

✪ Entertainment p159

🛍 Shopping p159

Our Writer

Fionn Davenport

Irish by birth and conviction, Fionn has spent the last two
decades focusing on the country of his birth and his nearest
neighbour, England, which he has written about extensively
for Lonely Planet. In between writing gigs he has lived in Paris
and New York, where he was an editor, actor, bartender and
whatever else paid the rent. For the last 15 years or so he's
also presented a series of programmes on Irish radio, most
recently as host of *Inside Culture* on RTÉ Radio 1. A couple of
years ago he moved to the northwest of England, where he
lives with his partner, Laura, and their car, Trevor.

Published by Lonely Planet Global Limited
CRN 554153
4th edition – Feb 2018
ISBN 9781 78657 342 1
© Lonely Planet 2018   Photographs © as indicated 2018
10 9 8 7 6 5 4 3 2 1
Printed in Malaysia

Although the authors and Lonely Planet
have taken all reasonable care in preparing
this book, we make no warranty about the
accuracy or completeness of its content
and, to the maximum extent permitted,
disclaim all liability arising from its use.

All rights reserved. No part of this publication may be copied, stored in a retrieval system, or transmitted in any form by
any means, electronic, mechanical, recording or otherwise, except brief extracts for the purpose of review, and no part of
this publication may be sold or hired, without the written permission of the publisher. Lonely Planet and the Lonely Planet
logo are trademarks of Lonely Planet and are registered in the US Patent and Trademark Office and in other countries.
Lonely Planet does not allow its name or logo to be appropriated by commercial establishments, such as retailers,
restaurants or hotels. Please let us know of any misuses: lonelyplanet.com/ip.